MEN, WOMEN AND SOCIETY

The untold stories of truths and lies
about the modern world

ADITYA GUPTA

INDIA • SINGAPORE • MALAYSIA

Copyright © Aditya Gupta 2023
All Rights Reserved.

ISBN

Paperback: 979-8-89067-803-4

Hardcase: 979-8-89133-847-0

"10 years of schooling

Four years of university education

Get a college degree and find a nice job

Buy an average house and a car

Then wait 40 years to die

That's not what life is meant for"

- Aditya Gupta

CONTENTS

ACKNOWLEDGEMENTS

A heartfelt shoutout to the amazing individuals whose profound knowledge, insightful mindsets, and deep understanding served as the guiding light for my book's creation. Your wisdom and support transformed my ideas into a literary reality. Grateful for your contributions that enriched every page!

- **ANDREW TATE**
- **TRISTAN TATE**
- **MYRON GAINES**
- **JUSTIN WALLER**
- **PATRICK BET DAVID**
- **SNEAKO**
- **JUST PEARLY THINGS**
- **FRESH & FIT PODCAST**
- **WHATEVER PODCAST**

SPECIAL THANKS

I'd like to express my sincere gratitude to our parents for their unwavering support and encouragement throughout this journey. Your guidance and sacrifices have been invaluable, and your love has been the foundation upon which this book was built. Thank you for believing in me and for being a source of inspiration. Your contribution to my life is immeasurable.

Prepare yourself because you are about to start a journey to become the best version of yourself. You will acquire information about the world's reality and falsity. Only a handful of people in this world are willing to put their lives in danger and are coming forward to expose the lies and realities that have been kept from you despite being there in front of your eyes. We will discover a lot about men, women, and society as a whole. The complex factors that affect our lives and relationships are clarified in this book. The complexity of gender roles, cultural expectations, and the challenges men and women encounter in negotiating these constructions have all been covered in these pages. Let's unite together so that we can make the world a better place to live.

1

MEN AND WOMEN

Before I convey my thoughts, let's discuss what men and women are in society. In this modern-day environment, we perceive one another as adversaries and rivals. Instead of understanding and listening to one another, we see each other through the enemy's eyes. Our conflict not only has a terrible impact on society, but it is also producing a negative environment in our surroundings. It even has a detrimental impact on our children's minds, as a result of which unfavourable thoughts begin to emerge. The world is simply imposing expectations on all of us, stating that you should do this because you are a man and that you should do this because you are a woman, but we have forgotten that we are, first and foremost, we are humans and that God created us to spread love amongst each other. I used to be an atheist, but I began to believe in God again for a variety of reasons; therefore, I'll provide my perspective throughout the book based on my beliefs. By linking you to God, I will do my best to reveal to you the reality of the world.

EQUAL BUT DIFFERENT

It is foolish and idiotic to argue that men and women are the same because, if we were identical, then God would not have created us separately and given us different qualities, powers, characteristics, looks, and, most significantly, our genitals (a human's intimate part). We should be treated equally, but we are not the same, and that is something we must accept. We each have a unique set of chromosomes, genetics, structures, and features. There is nothing similar between the two of us. There is a significant reason why God has separated us. From a biological standpoint, we have unique qualities and attributes.

Men and women have diverse physical, mental, and emotional qualities that distinguish them from one another. We cannot change the fact that we are all here for some purpose; we all have roles and responsibilities that we must embrace and fulfil as human beings.

UPCOMING OF NEW ERA

We have been playing distinct roles based on our gender since the dawn of humanity. Men used to protect and provide for their families, while women used to remain at home and care for them. The duties and expectations that are connected with each gender have been shaped by social, cultural, and historical considerations between the two of us, but the situation has changed. The world is evolving, and in today's advanced culture, women are receiving equal rights. Both of us have access to the same number of facilities, resources, and opportunities. It's true that there are still some areas where things haven't changed, but the world is waking up and realising that women deserve the same rights and treatment as men.

DIFFERENCE BETWEEN MEN AND WOMEN

In this section, we shall discuss the physical, mental, and emotional differences between men and women. Recognizing that a more significant topic is coming next, let's approach it properly. Men are more masculine, stronger, taller, have a low pitch, a heavy voice, and a wider chest; women are more feminine, weaker, shorter, with a high pitch, a sharper voice, wider hips, and a low center of gravity.

EXPERIENCES ARE WHAT DIFFERENTIATE US

There are numerous other things from which you can comprehend the distinction. As humans, we are not born with innate programming like machines. Instead, our experiences shape us and influence how we perceive and navigate life. However, it's important to note that as we progress and mature, our individual lived experiences can vary greatly from one another. We differ from one another due to our many traits, flaws, issues, environments, educational backgrounds, and—most significantly—the various repercussions and events that we experience in life.

THERE IS A REASON BEHIND IT

Since it is a man's duty to provide for and defend his family, men are inherently stronger and more powerful than women. A man has a responsibility to overcome challenges for his family. The reason why women are made to be weaker and gentler than men is because it is their responsibility to safeguard their families spiritually. It is the responsibility of a woman to look after, support, and foster a healthy atmosphere within the family (I'm not being sexist; I'm only describing how society has seen the obligations according to genders). Personally, I have nothing against any woman who works hard and succeeds in life. Therefore, don't think I'm a sexist who hates women.

When a man becomes a father, he must be strong in every way so that his child will be inspired by him to grow up to be a brave, fearless, and successful man like him. In contrast, when a woman becomes a mother, she must be soft, kind, and gentle so that her child can receive the best upbringing and learn from her that it is important to be kind and loving to the world when needed.

UPBRINGING PLAYS A MAJOR ROLE

Both of us have various roles that we play from the beginning to the end of our lives in different historical periods. As we get older, parents advise males to be brave, powerful, and strong because they are boys, while telling girls that they should be kind, soft, and gentle because they are daughters. Therefore, our development in upbringing about our responsibilities and how to fulfil them occurs throughout this time.

PHYSICAL DIFFERENCES ARE NOT RANDOM

There is a tremendous physical difference between men and women. On average, men are taller and larger than women; men have higher muscle mass and less body weight, while women have less muscle mass and more body weight; men have high levels of testosterone, which is linked to muscle growth, aggression, and the growth of facial hair; while women have oestrogen, which is linked to the menstrual cycle, pregnancy, and lactation.

You might be wondering why I started detailing it in such detail at this point and what the need is for it.

In essence, I aim to demonstrate that these qualities are neither man-made nor manufactured. We are born with every feature; thus, they are not random. We are physically different from one another for a reason, and it is crucial that you understand this seriously. We are designed to fulfil each other's needs and become stronger in each other's areas of weakness.

NECESSARY FOR EACH OTHER

We must never lose sight of the fact that we are here first and foremost to share love and peace as humans. Most people wish to look all over the world for their true love. In the end, we get married to the person we think is best and most ideal for us. Occasionally, disagreements arise in our personal lives after marriage as a result of having different perspectives and life choices. In order to fix the issue, we should try to understand and listen to one another rather than hate each other.

We must understand that even though we are different from each other, we were created for one another. You cannot deny the fact that we are essential to each other and that our dependence on one another is necessary for human existence.

HARSH CIRCUMSTANCES DEVELOP MENTAL STRENGTH

I believe that most men are generally mentally stronger because they experience more problems, trauma, and difficult situations than women, which causes their minds to gradually develop to handle more stress. Men handle stressful situations more effectively than women, as has been observed in several scenarios.

However, we cannot precisely determine who is mentally stronger because mental strength varies from person to person.

It depends on how many difficulties, challenges, and issues a person has encountered in life. An individual becomes more psychologically robust when life gets harder. How well a person handles challenges and tribulations reveals how psychologically strong they are. Actually, each person has a different level of mental toughness. From my perspective, men experience more trauma in life than women do. Trauma affects both men and women, but because women are more expressive than men, trauma can have a greater detrimental impact on women's brains.

UPBRINGING + EXPERIENCES = EMOTION

We now go on to the emotional part, where we will discuss the emotional distinctions between men and women. Since feelings are essential for comprehending one's circumstances, our ability to feel one another is the reason we are called humans. As a result, men and women react differently to situations due to emotions.

I won't get too deep here, but let me give you an example: If a woman witnesses a person or an animal in pain or in a distressed state, she will feel more pain and respond to the situation more emotionally than a man would because women are portrayed as more nurturing and empathetic, whereas men are portrayed as less emotional and more cerebral. Women are not innately more emotional than men.

KEY FACTORS PLAYS VITAL ROLE

Individuals' emotional expression and experience can differ vastly regardless of gender. The assumption that women are more emotional than men is founded on preconceptions and societal expectations rather than scientific data. It is essential to identify that emotional experiences and beliefs fluctuate from person to person and can be influenced by a variety of factors such as personal upbringing, cultural setting, socialization, and individual differences.

In essence, emotion differs from person to person, depending greatly on the circumstances and surroundings in which the specific one was nurtured. The experiences, challenges, and issues a person has encountered in life have a profound impact on his or her mental state. Different upbringing and experiences create different people.

HOW EMOTIONAL ARE WE?

The way a person responds to a specific scenario may quickly reveal how they are feeling (the response can take many different forms, such as unhappy, pleased, unexpected, etc.). Women are "allowed" to show emotion, but they must do it in the correct way and at the appropriate intensity. Men are "not accepted" to be emotional, but they nonetheless display the same emotions. Women tend to express their feelings more openly since they are emotional beings by nature.

However, this does not imply that males lack feelings. Studies indicate that men and women both feel emotions to a similar degree. Additionally, it depends on the sort of feelings we're discussing. In general, men tend to show their feelings less than women do. It also depends on our upbringing since infancy.

WE ARE RAISED IN A DEFINITE WAY

Boys are raised to be strong, bold, and fearless. They are also taught from an early age that men don't weep, which naturally trains their minds to repress their emotions. Girls are trained to be soft, kind, and gentle; they are also taught that it is okay to weep. It trains her mind to be more expressive in terms of expressing feelings.

Men don't cry is one of the finest things that guys are taught, in my opinion, because I feel that a man should never be overly emotional or reveal his vulnerability to anyone since the world does not appreciate weak men. Emotional men are hazardous because they lack control, and a man becomes harmful to society when he lacks emotional control. Emotions are a crucial component of being human, and both men and women experience a wide range of emotions, including happiness, sorrow, rage, fear, and love.

On the other hand, societal norms and gender roles frequently impact how emotions are expressed and perceived.

Cultural conditioning can have an impact on how people of different genders express their emotions, giving the appearance that women are more emotional. But, in the end, we both conclude that men and women experience emotions on the same level. Thus, we discussed the differences between men and women in physical, mental, and emotional ways.

UNCONDITIONAL AND CONDITIONAL LOVE

The civilization and culture we have been living in for hundreds of years contain one harsh fact that most people overlook: men are only loved conditionally, whereas women are loved unconditionally. It is a real statement that everyone should accept since men need to prove themselves and have a specific position, money, power, and lifestyle.

You will only be appreciated and liked if you have these qualities. You can observe these types of scenarios in your house and even in your surroundings if you look closely. Actually, it is not anyone's fault, but this is how things have been for a long time, and you cannot alter it overnight.

NO CONDITIONS ATTACHED

Women are loved unconditionally, with no conditions attached. She will always be adored, regardless of her social status or influence on society as a whole.

For instance, Sarah is a 19-year-old student at a university who comes from an ordinary household and isn't very attractive. The second girl's name is Emily, and although she is also 19 years old, she is stunningly attractive and comes from a wealthy family. Hence, despite her appearance and social standing, Sarah, the first girl, used to receive attention, care, support, and affection everywhere she went, including in her class, library, streets, pubs, and clubs. While Emily—who is stunning and comes from a wealthy family—will unquestionably receive more love, support, and attention than Sarah, the main point I was trying to make was that, regardless of whether you are attractive, wealthy, or famous, if you are a girl, you will always receive attention and affection. Women are born with value, while men have to create it.

CHOICE IS YOURS!

It is simple for women to find a guy; simply go into your inbox and choose the person according to your choice, or simply ask for any guy's phone number. I assure you that 99% of the time you will get the man you want.

In today's environment, it is much easier for a female to be lavished with care, affection, and attention. Almost every female has at least one guy in her inbox waiting for her response. In essence, what I was trying to say is that it is almost impossible for a female to go through life without being loved in modern society; it seems extremely rare. No guy will ask you to pay the bills and expenses; no one will expect anything from you; and your mistakes will be neglected (so it is basically unconditional).

GAME OF EXPECTATION

There are no expectations or conditions imposed on you; it is simply "No expectation, No condition." Men just ask for their wives' loyalty and support; in contrast, women have high expectations from their husbands. It is a basic norm, and there are numerous instances in our household and society.

If a man works, his entire family expects him to work hard in order to make money and improve his family's situation. He would be appreciated only if he was making money and maintaining a standing in his family and society; however, if a woman remains at home, the only thing expected of her is to take care of her family and home. She will still be loved and cared for because of her inherent value, regardless of whether she isn't doing her duties effectively.

If a woman no longer wishes to work, she is free to do so at any moment since she is a woman. She will not be under any pressure to earn money, and she will be free to leave at any moment because it is a man's responsibility to provide for his wife and family. Family and society won't condemn her, but if a guy does the same, the result will be very different. He will be scrutinized in every way, mocked, disgraced, despised, and labelled worthless for his choice.

DON'T FORGET YOU ARE A "MAN"

For the man who feels it is unfair and unjust, I simply want to say one thing to you: you are a loser, and you have lost the dignity to call yourself a man.

Keep in mind that it is your responsibility as a man to take care of your family and protect them; you are accountable and liable for them. It is her choice to decide whether she want to work or not but you as a man have no option. It is her decision whether or not to work, but you, as a guy, have no option. You must embrace reality; you cannot change how the world works. A guy must meet a number of requirements in order to be accepted by society. To be liked, he must overcome several obstacles.

Every single woman has different expectations for the type of man she wants. Women will offer you a long list of qualities they look for in a man, including things like intelligence, bravery, height, strength, maturity, income, and success. When asked what sort of woman they seek, the majority of men would only list two qualities: a woman who is trustworthy and beautiful.

NOW OR NEVER, BECOME VALUABLE

The world is much more competitive for guys out there; a man must outcompete other men to obtain something. As a man, you must build your own value and importance in order to be appreciated, and your value is determined by your level of accomplishment in life. A man is not born with innate value; he must fight and battle his entire life to obtain the affection women inherit.

> *"Women, children, and dogs are loved unconditionally. A man is only loved under the condition that he provides something."*
>
> *– Chris Rock*

The aforementioned line illustrates the fact that a guy has to provide in order to be valued. Everyone should understand that this world is cruel and that humans were made in such a manner that we always desire affection and care. At some point in their lives, both men and women need love. Most of you are unaware of the fact that more than 90% of men secretly desire love and affection in their lives.

BIND WITH CONDITIONS

Since we are all in constant competition with one another and life is a game of skill, the majority of men manage to exist without receiving any attention, respect, love, or care. As a result, each guy has a condition that must be met at a certain point in order for him to receive what he desires. Men must establish their worth and attain a specific position in order to get the same level of affection and care that women are given as an inheritance. As the saying goes, "where there is an expectation, there is a condition."

Men must perform specific duties and live up to certain standards in order to be loved and cherished by their families, partners, and society at large. This might involve giving financial assistance, assuming leadership responsibilities, and displaying fortitude and endurance in the face of hardship.

ACCEPT THE HARSH REALITY

The majority of men never receive a rose until they die or are initially approached by a woman. Since men are also human beings, they also need care and affection. You cannot ignore or avoid the harsh reality that men have to face; the truth will remain the truth even if you choose not to accept it.

I believe that a man only receives unconditional love from his mother and father throughout his entire life. No matter what happens, his parents will always adore him, but as he gets older, they will begin to have expectations of him. When a boy reaches the age of 18, he starts to get adult treatment and is expected to grow into a man. Conditions start being imposed on him from every direction in all sorts of ways. With age, expectations begin to increase gradually.

SAME SITUATION, DIFFERENT OUTCOMES

In the same manner as before, I'll use an example here: Jack is a 20-year-old boy from a middle-class household who is intelligent and charming. A different youngster named Sam, who is similarly 20 years old, average-looking, and not very intellectual, comes from a wealthy family and is well-known and influential.

The circumstances will not play out as they did in the girl's case in this instance.

Sam was lavished with love, care, and attention from the females, despite the fact that he wasn't even gorgeous. Sam was wealthy, well-known, and a powerful guy (he has value and status in society that are more significant than looks). In contrast, Jack was brilliant and charming but rarely received attention, love, or care from the females. Try to realize that you won't be loved until you have something to offer.

IT IS WHAT IT IS

One of the most accurate things I've ever heard is that only women, children, and dogs are loved unconditionally. A man is only loved if he provides something. I believe a man should never forget this statement because it will serve as a constant reminder that his relevance will only be determined by his accomplishments and position. A man has to succeed in his life in order to be considered valuable.

You can experience the power and the love you've been searching for a very long time if you are financially secure, physically fit, and possess certain social standing. Imagine how miserable your life would be if you didn't receive any kind of attention, love, or care. Instead of thinking about a lifetime or a whole year, let's merely imagine one month. I guarantee that any modern woman will experience trembling in both her body and mind after thinking about that scenario. Imagine how miserable and gloomy life would be if no one gave a damn about you. Think about how a man can sometimes live his entire life without any of these things. How painful and lonely his existence would be, suffering all by himself with no one to share it with.

YOUR PRESENT DECISION WILL DETERMINE YOUR FUTURE

We must acknowledge that although we cannot alter the way the world functions, we can alter our own lives and mindsets in order to achieve the life we have always desired. By becoming valuable, you can find the love that has been completely absent from your life throughout the entire time. Women and children are intrinsically deserving of love just by virtue of their existence, whereas men must earn affection and love through their deeds and accomplishments.

There are many guys who believe that we deserve to be loved unconditionally and that it should not be contingent on predefined gender roles and expectations. I just want to say to all these men that if you want to change how the world thinks, the first thing is that it cannot be changed in a short period of time, and even in the best-case scenario, it will take at least hundreds of years.

Therefore, instead of acting like victims, you all need to work rigorously to earn that love and care, because that is how the world operates. Always keep in mind that you have responsibilities and duties as a man. A true guy doesn't ever make excuses.

2

REJECT MODERNITY EMBRACE MASCULINITY

In order to actively engage in the ongoing discussion, it is imperative that you possess a comprehensive understanding of the terms that are being discussed.

Masculinity: qualities and attributes regarded as characteristic of men

Modernity: the quality or condition of being modern (the meaning changes with context).

Therefore, it could be said that the term "masculinity" refers to the traits and features seen to be specific to men. Men's social behavior in society is dictated by a set of rules and standards known as masculinity. Various definitions and interpretations exist in the realm of what encompasses masculinity, with societal norms and cultural expectations playing a significant role in shaping these understandings.

"Being a male is a matter of birth. Being a man is a matter of choice."

– Edwin Louis Cole

IMPORTANCE OF MASCULINITY

It dictates that men must always be self-sufficient, courageous, tough, and emotionally strong in order to maintain their status and respect as men. In the modern world, this is what it really means to be a man. A guy needs to work on himself if he lacks these qualities, since the world is cruel and unforgiving to everyone. If you refuse to acknowledge that every man must be masculine, you are still a weak-minded boy. You are downplaying the significance of being ready before a crisis knocks on the door.

Masculinity encourages men to be bold, tough, and emotionally resilient because the world is a prison, and it is critical for you to recognize that it is all about survival of the fittest. It is vital for men to be masculine since it has always been a man's job to defend his wife and family. How can you fulfil your responsibilities as a man if you are not masculine?

THEY DON'T WANT WHAT THEY CLAIM

A weak and cowardly man cannot provide protection to anyone. Many women in today's culture claim that we need a kind, sensitive, and nice man, but the fact is that they just desire these types of men for dating and pleasure.

When it comes time to choose the sort of person they want to marry, their perspectives and preferences shift dramatically. They claim that I need a guy who will take care of me, protect me, and provide food and shelter for my family. Every woman needs a guy who is physically, financially, and emotionally strong because they believe it is the male's role and obligation to provide and protect. They understand and recognize that they cannot spend their entire lives with an immature and weak individual who is incapable of carrying out his obligations as a man.

Every woman desires a spouse who is capable of carrying out all of the obligations and tasks that come with marriage.

PURPOSEFULLY PLANNED GAMEPLAY

Everyone is aware of reality, but the matrix creates and sustains this worldview in people's minds. The elites (global leaders) want to weaken all men in order to effortlessly keep their grip over the planet. The term "toxic masculinity" did not exist in prior times.

Although I cannot guarantee it, I believe that the majority of you may have come across this phrase for the first time via the news or on social media. All these things, such as mainstream media, social media apps, and companies, are controlled by the individuals who run the world behind closed doors. As a result of prior planning, the term "Toxic masculinity" suddenly became popular. You might be wondering why they'd overpower it at this point. There is an easy answer. If you want to break any civilization or country, simply make men weak, since men are the backbone. As a result, they seized control by instilling hatred between both sexes.

Why were these topics not previously discussed?

ARE YOU REALLY LOOKING FOR EQUALITY?

Development and progress were still occurring and increasing over these years, but suddenly, topics and agendas such as toxic masculinity, feminism, femininity, masculinity, and misuse of authority came into the spotlight. I do not oppose feminism, but I do oppose fake feminism (actions or statements that appear to support feminist principles but are not actually grounded in a genuine belief in gender equality).

All genders should have equal rights and opportunities, according to feminism. Therefore, according to this definition, I am a feminist because I believe that women should have the same rights and opportunities as men. In both Western and Indian civilizations, women have the same rights as men. If you look closely and compare, you will find that women have more benefits than men in modern society. You cannot consider yourself as a feminist if you wish to establish dominance.

CHOOSE THE GOD'S GIVEN PATH

The terms, Masculine and feminine were designed primarily for men and women. God has created us different from each other for a reason: A man should be masculine because men typically play more masculine roles in society, whereas a woman should be feminine because women often play more feminine ones.

If you want guys to be feminine, it should not be acceptable because the phrase was developed for women. It is not realistic for a guy to change into a woman and defy nature. I find it difficult to comprehend why people support and embrace men who identify themselves as women; in my opinion, this kind of behavior weakens society as a whole. Therefore, it is essential that we both stick to the paths that have been laid out for us. A man should be masculine and a woman should be feminine, because in the end, it is the only thing that matters. According to me, A woman should be feminine as well as masculine. She should know when to display her masculine side since there are moments in life when masculine characteristics are required.

NO OPTION LEFT

The only way a guy can fulfil his responsibilities as a parent, husband, brother, and son is by being completely masculine. As a guy, you should be able to handle any kind of situation. You will never see a gorgeous and clever lady wed a weak and feminine guy because what they actually desire is a strong, courageous, and successful man who can defend and provide for her and her family. Therefore, if you truly comprehend what masculinity implies, it is not only healthy but also non-toxic.

Masculinity encourages men to feel a certain way and still complete tasks regardless of how they feel, or ignore how they feel. The greatest and most incredible people you've ever seen in history also weren't motivated to do the things they did, but they knew that they had to perform them in order to demonstrate respect for their dignity and moral obligation.

IT IS NOT OK TO ACCEPT THEIR AGENDA

According to me, it should not matter to a man if he is feeling happy or sad; he should do the things he is supposed to do. As a man, you have a responsibility to uphold your dignity. When I say that we should reject modernity and embrace masculinity, I mean that we should oppose modernity's attempts to weaken men and women in every aspect. Social media and the press are doing their hardest to weaken men physically, emotionally, and mentally. They are training and shaping our brains to think that it is OK to be weak, that guys may weep, that it is OK to be feminine, that it isn't necessarily a man's responsibility to defend the family, etc. Just try to picture a man uttering these things. What a wimp he'd be.

SHOW MEN THE MIRROR

If any woman is reading this, please respond to this question honestly: Which of these two would you like to marry? The first guy is strong, bold, well-established, defends you, and upholds his obligations as a man. In contrast, the second man is frail, kind, and needy; he is frightened and not well-established. I don't actually require an answer; I already know that most women would choose option 1, and you are also aware of your own preference. Because if you can't marry someone like that, don't encourage him to be like that.

I sincerely request any woman to refrain from telling a child or a man that it's okay to be weak and feminine. Tell them outright that they are unable, immature, and unsuccessful and that they must change because when one man presents another man with the facts, he often takes them in a humorous way. However, I'm confident that if a woman tells a guy the truth, he will take it seriously since the words will have a distinctive impact on him.

FEMININE SIDE IS BEAUTIFUL

You'll never hear a man telling a girl or woman, "I need you to be strong, masculine, and powerful. A man always loves his woman to be feminine because women always seem more attractive when they are feminine.

Men desire women to be soft, kind, delicate, and sensitive so that they can offer the love, support, care, and tranquilly that a guy requires from his lady. Men desire feminine women because they admire women who are delicate, kind, sensitive, soft, emotional, and caring. Because they are aware that being feminine will make them adored, most women strive to be feminine. If you don't believe me, just ask any male what kind of girl or woman he likes.

BOON AND CURSE

Modernity is a good thing, and it primarily comes through western culture in India. If you look, there are some things that were advantageous for our nation at one point, like modern medicine, technology, the education system, the banking system, transportation, and human rights, but in many ways, some things are so bad that they are gradually eating and destroying our country from the inside out, such as the loss of traditional skills, disrespecting elders, forgetting the Indian culture, hookup culture, an increase in violence, and environmental destruction.

SOCIAL MEDIA AND TECHNOLOGY COMES WITH "+" AND "-"

We will not discuss modernity as a whole in this article; instead, we'll choose a few issues that seem pertinent to our subject.

People used to know fewer people in their lifetime, meet fewer people, and be more honest and sincere about their lives and sentiments before the rise of social media and western culture. People now have access to a limitless number of connections because of advancements in technology. Despite the fact that individuals can now speak with people they have never met or known, there are also benefits and drawbacks to this.

In this topic, I'll be talking about how the hookup culture has spread to major cities in recent years and will eventually engulf all of India in the upcoming years.

ARE WE TAKING RIGHT TURN?

If we look at our parents (the 90s generation), I am sure that most of them didn't have a lot of relationships and didn't go on hundreds of dates before marrying each other, and the surprising thing is that their marriages were more successful than ours.

Most weddings were arranged within the caste, and we can observe that marriages were more successful in the past even though people used to meet a few months before the marriage. We are able to see that they used to live together until their last breath. Indeed, it is astonishing to find that love marriages are failing and divorce rates have risen within the past few decades. Divorces have already had a detrimental effect in the West, and India is also going to face it shortly.

WHY WEST IS FALLING?

In the West, divorce rates are at an all-time high, and most marriages nowadays end with divorce. Earlier divorce rates were fairly low, but in today's contemporary culture, they are now at a record-breaking level. In earlier times, people used to consider a lot before getting married, and parents' involvement was extremely important.

Even after knowing that parents have far more life experience than theirs and that they are aware of the potential issues that might arise in marriages down the road, children still seek relatively little parental participation. People no longer take enough time while selecting their life partner, nor do they consider talking about any future conflicts and concerns that can occur between them. In the West, children have the freedom to select their spouses and can engage in casual relationships. However, because we now meet and date many people before we get married, this modern trend may occasionally contribute to divorces because it exposes us to a wide variety of people and relationships.

As a result, we'll start evaluating and comparing our partner with each of them. Life is not perfect, and sometimes our companion cannot provide us with everything we want. When expectations are not satisfied in today's world, individuals start to look for alternatives rather than fixing the problem. Another reason for the high divorce rate in the West is that they believe in the concept of casual relationships. Casual relationships were meant for physical bonding and spending time with the opposite sex without the pressure of marriage.

MARRIAGES ARE NOT REAL ANYMORE

Marriage is all about giving 100% of oneself to one another. Many sacrifices have to be made in order to keep marriage alive. Understanding and supporting one another during stressful times is essential. It's heartbreaking to realize that both men and women have forgotten that they agreed to support and respect one another for the rest of their lives. People these days are immature and egoistic, which is causing marriages and families to fall apart. When two people are separated from each other, not only do they suffer, but their families suffer as well. I would like the citizens of India to reject this modernism because it has already begun to spread in our nation and is going to expand fast in the next few decades. I assure you that finding someone you can completely trust and love will become far more difficult in the upcoming years.

NOTE: A survey has revealed that 76% of Indian women and 61% of men don't think that infidelity is a sin or immoral. There are other contradictions too.

A good number of people say they have never been caught having an affair (81% men and 92% women). Even if some of them did get caught, for 77% of men and 62% of women, the discovery didn't lead to divorce. – The Times of India

The fact that divorce rates are low in India does not necessarily mean that the country is doing well. All of the statistics above demonstrate how much worse India's condition is presently and will be in a few years.

PERFECTION IS NOT REAL

Actually, the concept of soulmates is utterly ridiculous, not because you need to look for them all over the world but because you need to find someone who is completely perfect for you. Accept the fact that no one in this world is perfect. You don't need to find the ideal match, but you must find someone who can understand, love, and support you through your ups and downs. The concept of a perfect person is false; it is a fabrication created to raise people's expectations. A successful and happy relationship is something that you and your partner build together. It is essential to choose the right partner—someone who will add value to your family and kids.

ABANDON THE HOOKUPS CULTURE

People no longer desire to stay with a single individual because of the expanding hookups culture. In today's society, it is viewed as stupid and silly for a person to love, respect, and care for his mate. In the present world, having several partners and sleeping with a lot of people is considered cool and prideful.

However, I can assure you that this mentality is highly harmful to our society since it promotes cheating, disloyalty, and betrayal among the young generation It is one of the main reasons why individuals are reluctant to put their confidence in one another. For both men and women over the age of 30, I just have one question. Do you regret choosing to be with several partners at once? I'm not sure if you regret it or not, but I'm quite sure you've had a moment where you wished you'd been a regular person and focused on one person or one relationship at a time. You shouldn't have deceived and wounded the emotions of others.

Once in a while, we come to the realization that we need to put everything on hold in order to meet someone with whom we can calmly settle our lives. A woman looks for a spouse who will love her unconditionally, who will protect her, and who can create a happy family.

THE OUTCOME WILL BE CATASTROPHIC

Most guys in today's world are unaware of how quickly time is passing. They are unaware that in order to succeed in this difficult environment, you must put in a greater effort. You need to have a broad perspective; you cannot chase women for the rest of your life.

I am quite aware that I am referring to western culture, but I feel obligated to bring it up since I am aware of how much of our nation is an outcome of western culture. The day when India closely resembles the West is not too far off since everyone is being impacted by western culture. I have one message for both men and women who support and enjoy the hookup and cheating culture: one day you will desire to settle down, but you will realize that society as a whole has been ruined, making it difficult for you to find someone with whom you can spend the rest of your life. Finding a man and a woman who are worth the effort to become life partners will soon become challenging. Being a good husband and wife requires a lot of sacrifice and commitment.

PROMISCUITY IS SHAMED

Men are viewed in their future, whereas women are viewed in their past, not just in marriages but also in life as a whole. Women are judged for who they were in the past, whereas men are judged for who they will be in the future.

No one will criticize a man for having hundreds of women sleep with him, but the world and society will condemn a woman for doing the same. You must accept the hard realities of life and try to understand that life isn't fair. There has never been a woman who received praise or recognition for engaging in promiscuous behavior throughout the entire span of human civilization, extending back to the earliest records of human history. You must face the truth and exert all of your efforts in order to prove your worth as a real woman. Any ideology that supports multiple relationships and infidelity is something I despise since it wreaks havoc on other people's lives.

PEACE RESIDES WITH IN ONE

Our country as a whole is suffering from the effects of this culture. This sort of modernity needs to be rejected because it will eventually destroy our country. In actuality, finding peace requires committing to a lifetime with a single individual. It's a beautiful experience to be able to develop a happy, healthy family with your partner while continuing to love and protect them. Modernity has a lot to do with masculinity and femininity.

WEAKNESS IS UNACCEPTABLE

The second thing we should reject is the idea that men can be weak and sensitive. Every country and society need a guy who can provide and protect, as well as be brave and powerful in all aspects. You may have seen a number of videos on social media of westerners admitting that it is acceptable to be obese, that it is acceptable to change one's biological gender, that it is acceptable for men to wear makeup similar to that worn by women, and that it is acceptable for men to appear weak and feminine.

THEY ARE NOT ON YOUR SIDE

Have you ever considered how and why it is reaching us? You're right, it's because of news and media. Because the world is so vast, the only way to learn about what is happening around the globe is through the news and media.

People have always believed that the news they watch is accurate and beneficial for society as a whole, but the reality is actually quite the opposite. The government, which is controlled by elites, owns all media outlets and news organizations. Through the news and the media, they can easily manipulate people's thoughts and views. The best approach to influencing people's minds is to limit what they see and hear, because everyone in the world uses and consumes media. Since our minds are products of what we see and hear, it follows that if they have influence over what we consume, they must also have control over our minds. Everything you see is pre-planned; nothing is happening by accident.

MASCULINITY IS DYING

They are trying their best to weaken the male community by pushing these objectives. If men become frail and weak, it will be much simpler to govern any society or country since there will be no one to challenge them.

People at the top of the world can simply maintain their position and impose their norms on others without any opposition. In the West, for example, there are many recordings of men begging women to be with them, men licking women's shoes, men walking like dogs with a chain around their neck, and other heinous acts. Men are losing their self-esteem and honor these days; just to be with a woman who doesn't even care about him. It is not the woman's fault; a woman is not compelling any man to stay and stick with her; rather, it is the fault of men who do not respect themselves.

EGO AND AWARENESS OF SELF-WORTH ARE ESSENTIAL

I want all of the men to be fully prepared for the coming years. Develop into a true man. Be brave, have a strong ego, and never beg someone to stay in your life. The modern world is full of people who do not care about themselves.

Men are becoming weak, needy, helpless, cowardly, and shameless. They are willing to go to any extent in order to obtain a woman, even if it means sacrificing their self-respect. I know it is difficult to live without love, care, and attention, but try to understand, my brother, that you are broke, weak, and sensitive, and no one wants you, so first establish your own worth. Create your own value as a man in order to be respected and loved. Become the man that all women desire. No matter how attractive a woman is, you should always have a strong sense of self-worth and ego that you will never compromise in any situation (reject modernity, embrace your masculinity).

Few individuals in contemporary society are resisting modernism in order to uphold traditional masculinity. I want every man to be strong, powerful, bold, and tough in every way.

ARE YOU A MAN OF YOUR WORD?

If a man chooses a feminine path, he is not only dishonoring his ancestors but also himself by refusing to accept his responsibilities as a man. A man who is afraid to endure pain and suffering has no right to be called a man. Whenever a man chooses pleasure and satisfaction over his obligations, he should really be ashamed of himself. An average man does what he feels like doing, but a true man does what he is supposed to do; the choice is yours.

Most men do not realize how necessary it is for a man to be masculine. It is important for every man to discover the strength and potential of his body and intellect.

"No man has the right to be an amateur in the matter of physical training. It is a shame for a man to grow old without seeing the beauty and strength of which his body is capable."

— Socrates

The world must recognize the truth, and you must understand that weakness is never valued by the world. Reject modern ideology and become strong, brave, powerful, and fearless. The world is a tough place to survive; you never know who will attack you; therefore, you must learn to be unstoppable and resilient. Always be prepared for any possible consequences. You shouldn't promote violence, but you should be capable of doing it.

CURRENT WEST = FUTURE INDIA

I chose each of these subjects because I am aware of how influential the West has been on India. It might not be harming India right now, but it will likely have a larger impact on our nation in the future. Our nation has been influenced by the West over the past few decades. Everything from the clothes we wear to the food we eat to the education we receive to the technology we use is an outcome of the West. Modern ideologies are currently ruining the West, and similar things will soon begin to occur in the country as well; therefore, it is better to be prepared before the problem arrives. You cannot trust the media or the news; they are doing everything they can to spread false beliefs in order to achieve their evil objectives. There are enemies everywhere, wearing different masks; therefore, I would like every man and woman to wake up and see the reality of the world. The only way to avoid falling into the trap is to identify it.

IT IS NOT OK

The news and media are propagating a new contemporary agenda to undermine society, saying that "it's OK to stay as you are; you don't need to change." I'm going to link the context to the term "body shaming" here. People used to shame and make fun of fat people in the past, but now it is slowly being restricted in western schools to not allow children to tell the truth, which will soon reach here as well. I am against bullying, but I just want everyone to understand one thing: it is not okay to stay as you are.

IS IT HEALTHY OR NOT?

Every one of you can change yourself and become better every day in every aspect. Don't change for anyone else, but do it for yourself. The individuals in charge of the globe are spreading the message that it is immoral to criticize someone because they are fat, skinny, weak, or lazy. You all should understand that "body shaming is healthy."

You may now think that I am a terrible person who does not respect the sentiments of others. You should understand that body shaming is unhealthy for traits that you cannot change, such as height, skin color, and so on. However, body shaming is completely healthy in terms of things that can be modified, such as health and appearance. If people do not humiliate one another, the world would descend into anarchy, and everybody would be happy to remain as they are. If this occurs, a person who has built himself through hard labor would be rendered insignificant. Many people who have transformed their lives say, "I used to be obese, and people used to bully and make fun of me, and that's why I changed myself." Does not it demonstrate that body shaming is literally beneficial to individuals who wish to transform themselves?

SMALL CHANGES CREATE GREAT IMPACT

I guarantee that if you start working on yourself, people will start to see you as a leader and will start to respect you. Try to acknowledge that you are not unattractive; the problem is that you are not currently your best self.

Most of the time, those who believe they are unattractive are mistaken. I want you to understand that if you start to hit the gym and work on yourself financially, your appearance and personality will change completely. People will start to look at you with respect and admiration, and you will begin to appear much more appealing. The only things you need to modify are your clothing sense and communication abilities. By developing these two things, you will notice a significant improvement in yourself. Try to realize that it is not okay to stay as you are; there is always room for growth in your life. It's critical to constantly enhance your physical and mental health. I want every man and woman to strive to be the best versions of themselves. You only have one life, so how can you not want to be the best version of yourself?

EITHER THIS OR THAT

You cannot become perfect, but you may strive to be better than your previous self every day. As an example, imagine James, who was broke, overweight, and depressed. He wanted to change his life, but he was not dedicated enough to work for it. He had been depressed for a long time, but he never tried to figure out why. What If he changes his way of life, goes to the gym six days a week, hustles for his business, takes on an extra job, and works hard every day. By modifying his lifestyle, the same individual who had been overweight, broke, and depressed can become physically fit, financially free, and well-settled. He now has two alternatives in life: he can either stay obese and poor or he can improve himself and become wealthy.

<u>**NOTE:**</u> Never be satisfied with what you have in life. Satisfaction kills greatness. You only have one life, and you want to live it mediocrely. Living your life as an ordinary person is embarrassing and degrading. If a person doesn't have any goals, aspirations, or dreams in life, then he is simply a body ready to pass away. I don't understand how you don't have the desire to become an exceptional person. Look in the mirror and recognize your genuine potential. Your better self is asking you to come over and take the first step toward changing your life.

MOTIVATION IS NOT REAL

Remember one thing: Motivation isn't real. You don't need motivation to do anything or conquer anything; discipline and consistency are all it takes. Motivation in and of itself is a scam; motivation makes a person weak and creates a dependency habit, but discipline makes a person strong and independent. You cannot be constantly driven to accomplish things; instead, you must be disciplined. Discipline is what makes you get things done, even when you don't want to. Embrace the things that help you become a better version of yourself.

I believe that everyone should follow these three rules

Rule #1: Never be satisfied. Always have hunger within yourself.

Rule #2: Progress always takes place outside of comfort zone.

Rule #3: You have two options. one day, or day one.

WHAT ARE YOU DOING WITH YOUR LIFE?

More than 99 percent of people are aware that they are not performing or putting forth their best effort. One of the most essential things you can do is eliminate negativity and bad habits from your life. If you have self-sabotaging habits like procrastination, self-doubt, or perfectionism, you should be concerned. These patterns can hinder your personal growth and prevent you from reaching your goals. It is important to recognize and address these patterns in order to move forward. Stay focused and devoted; life has more to offer than you may imagine. Always set challenges for yourself. Never be happy with what you have in life; there is always something greater waiting for you. Never give up trying. Give up a few years to enjoy the rest of your life, or sacrifice the rest of your life to enjoy a few years. The choice is yours, champion.

GREATER SACRIFICE = GREATER REWARD

Men in today's society want to lead successful lives that are free from restrictions, but many do not want to make the sacrifices required to get there. There is not a single man on the planet who is successful and has not sacrificed anything in his life. The greater the sacrifice the greater the reward. Everything in life has a cost; pay the price and take it. The more successful you get, the harder and more stressful life becomes, since great power also comes with huge responsibility.

YOU ARE RUNNUNG OUT OF TIME; AN EXCUSE IS NOT AN OPTION

Modernity has blinded modern men by making them weak and distracted. There are thousands of men out there who are living their lives without any purpose or goal. Most people are unaware of how rapidly time passes; therefore, you must decide what you want from life as soon as possible. You will reach a point in your life when you will sit in the chair in your home and realize that it is already too late. You'll regret not having achieved greatness and success in life. Do not let the media and the matrix trick you into thinking it is acceptable to remain depressed and sad.

You don't realize that, as a guy, you've already wasted too much time in your life while being unhappy and depressed. How can you just sit back and make excuses when you are not yet successful? Grow up and become a man of words. Always remember A true gentleman never makes excuses. Reject modernity and embrace masculinity.

3

WHAT IT TAKES TO BE A MAN

Before discussing how to become a man, you must first understand what it takes to be a man. When you are a youngster under the age of five, you will not be told anything and will not be subjected to any pressure. Many people believe that there is no pressure on children until they are 12 or 13 years old, but they fail to realize that a child does not spend all of his time with his parents.

REALITY OF CHILDHOOD

When a youngster reaches the age of 5–6 years, he begins to meet new friends, talk to other people, and listen to his teachers. Once the children enter school, they are taught from that time that they must study hard and work on themselves because if they do not, they will become like them (beggars, trash pickers, et cetera).

As we grow older, we begin to feel pressured and coerced not just by our parents but also by society and a large number of individuals. Parents say that I don't ever force my kids. They say that I know he is not under pressure. I'd want to ask everyone whether they've ever attempted to talk to their child or if they've ever sat down and invited him to share his thoughts and issues as a friend. I am certain that you never asked your child if there was anything upsetting him or her; parents hardly ask their children what they truly want to accomplish with their lives.

DARK TRUTH ABOUT INDIA

This has been happening in India for a long time; when a child is born, parents already decide what they want their child to become before naming him or her. 90% of the time, youngsters are unable to communicate their choices to their parents. Each youngster wants to express, "I have a dream; I want to pursue my ambition; I want to do X thing." Even if they express their feelings, they are usually punished or terrified, and only a few parents allow their children to completely follow their own goals. These are issues that nearly every young person in the country faces. We'll talk about boys and men since this is about "what it takes to be a man."

HARSH REALITY BEHIND IT

On the one hand, society instructs people not to underestimate women, but on the other, they tell their son that even if his sister does not pursue an education, she will still find a husband. But this attitude is changing now, and I'm glad about it since it means that more parents are thinking seriously about their daughters' education and planning to marry her to someone who will treat her right.

It is true that if a woman is attractive, whether or not she has a good education, she will be able to marry someone from a prosperous household. But a man constantly has the pressure and stress in his head that if he does not succeed, no one will appreciate him, understand him, support him, or marry him. You cannot argue the fact that a man of little value cannot wed a woman of enormous value, but a woman of little value can wed a guy of immense value simply because of her beauty. I'm sorry to say that, but you are currently nothing but useless if you are not making a good living, have no prestige, and have no value even at the age of 24 or 25. A guy needs to prove himself at all times throughout his life.

You must create your own value as a man since you are not born with any intrinsic worth in this world. This is your biggest male strength, if you give it some thought.

VALUE YOUR TIME

I don't believe any guy can truly fail in his life if he works extremely hard, doesn't waste time, develops himself, and works on his flaws. Understand that you don't have enough time left to construct yourself from the ground up. The world is extremely competitive, especially for men. You may not realize it, but you are in constant competition every second. Someone is becoming better than you. While you are wasting your time scrolling through your phone, someone is becoming better every day.

People complain about how unfair the world is to them after squandering their entire day doing nothing worthwhile. You have no idea how competitive the world is for a man. I need to show all people, especially men, that your life is damn hard, and if you think you have enough time, you are wrong, my brother. Time always flies if you don't catch up with it, and if you don't believe me, ask people between the ages of 45 and 50. They will tell you the truth: each person says that they might have been a better person if they had not wasted their valuable time.

DIFFERENCE BETWEEN TWO OF THEM

In today's world, you have a lot to conquer because the majority of modern men are distracted. Here are two examples of men: The first man is 25 years old and has spent his whole youth wandering around the city, running behind females, dating, clubbing, partying. He is a lazy, overweight, and broke individual. The second man is likewise 25 years old, but he spent his prime years studying hard in university, hustled in his side business, developed his personality, and learned new skills. He is a wealthy, physically strong, and well-established man enjoying a high-class lifestyle. You can either become first man or second man, Choice is yours.

YOU ARE RESPONSIBLE FOR YOURSELF

As a man, you should accept that who you are and where you are in life is entirely due to you. Weak individuals blame others for their shortcomings. I understand I'm being tough here, but remember this:

no one compelled you to smoke, drink alcohol, or use drugs; the decision was entirely yours. Nobody compelled you to get a partner and spend all of your time with her instead of focusing on yourself.

Nobody compelled you to sit at home all day like a slacker or prevented you from going to the gym; the decision was entirely yours. Nobody forced you to spend time with your friends when you might have worked on yourself or studied hard; the decision was yours. Even after knowing these facts, how can you blame your failure on previous events, consequences, or other people? You are also aware of the fact that it is just an excuse to cover up your mistakes and decisions. Your decisions will determine where you end up in life, whether they are major or minor. Every choice you make will affect how your future turns out. You should be aware of your priorities; it is critical to identify what is essential to you at present.

Every man and woman who reads this book should clear their lives from all distractions and negativity. Work toward the things in life that are truly important to you by investing every day with all of your energy. It's always a person's decision to be average. Don't be average; average is your enemy.

"He who says he can and he who says he can't are both usually right."

– Confucius

CHOOSE YOUR PATH

You, as a guy, must select which one you want to be. Life is difficult for men, but if you work with focus and discipline, it can be far different than what you think. There is still so much to accomplish and enjoy in life. Human life is a precious gift; do not waste it by settling for mediocrity.

As a man, you must suffer; remember that pain and trauma are what turn a boy into a man. You can't grow until you confront issues and obstacles in life. Progress is always made outside of one's comfort zone; become comfortable by being uncomfortable. God has sent us for a reason, yet many men are forgetting their true purpose in life. Your mission and God-given purpose should always be your top concerns. In today's environment, boys are frequently distracted by girls. I want all of the boys to become men as quickly as possible by removing any distractions from their lives, such as girls, smoking, drinking, toxic friends, and negative people.

Don't let anyone say anything negative about you since even minor things can have a big impact on your life.

ADVERSITY AND SUFFERING ARE ESSENTIAL

Struggle and pain are unavoidable for a guy, as I previously stated in the context that men will be loved under certain conditions; therefore, it is always a war for you with the man who works harder than you. Never believe that you are giving your best since satisfaction is an obstacle to your progress, therefore never be pleased. A boy becomes a man the moment he realizes that he has to become successful, get well settled, not waste time, and be in the best shape possible. Trauma and stress are necessary for a boy to evolve into a man because if he does not experience challenges and difficulties in life, he will not appreciate the value of anything. All of history's greatest men have experienced agony, suffering, trauma, and stress. Every challenge and adversity in life makes a guy stronger. It takes a lot of effort and determination to get to the top, which is why just 1% of individuals make it. To be successful in life, you must forge your own path.

KNOW YOUR RESPONSIBILITIES AND DUTIES

A man has responsibilities that he must fulfil. A man who refuses to embrace his responsibilities and runs away from them does not deserve to be called a man. Being a man is an honor and a source of pride that you must take with you for the rest of your life. God has given you great responsibilities and tasks since you are the chosen one; therefore, always look at them positively.

There are many responsibilities that a man should fulfil, but these are a few that I believe every man should understand and accept. A guy should always be physically and mentally strong since it is his responsibility to defend his loved ones. A man should shoulder the burden of any crisis or difficulty that his family is experiencing. A man should always open the car door for his girl; a man should always pay the bill; a man should always be prepared for the worst and never give up; a man should take care of, provide for, and protect his family; and there are many other things that it takes to become a man, so strive to improve every day. A man should always be willing to sacrifice his life for his loved ones. As a man, there is no shame in performing chivalrous acts for your woman. You should not care what others think; always remember that there is no shame in expressing your masculinity.

ADDITIONAL ADVICE - Take out your odds and work on them every day. There is always room for self-improvement, no matter how brilliant you are at your job. Explore your potential; there is a lot of physical and mental potential waiting for you. Choose a path, decide your purpose, and never look back again.

RISK IS NECESSARY TO SUCCEED

I want to inspire every man to take risks in life because many people don't realize that if you're not wealthy, you have nothing to lose. Imagine what would happen if you decided to start a side business with the $1,000 you had left in your pocket. Then, there are two possible outcomes: either you'll lose everything attempting to succeed or you'll become a millionaire with that hustle. There is no reward in life without risk; if you are not willing to risk even a small amount of money, then you do not deserve anything in life. A man who never takes risks will perpetually stay broke his entire life. If you never take a risk or make a move, your $1,000 will remain $1,000, but picture how embarrassing it will be to not even attempt even if there is a 1% chance of success. Imagine what type of life you will have if your hard work and perseverance pay off. Taking a risk is necessary, even if you only have a 1% chance of winning.

Always remember that each failure brings you one step closer to success. The ability to consistently learn and improve will eventually lead to results. Just wait for that one day when you will see your whole life completely change in front of your eyes. It takes a lot of dedication and hard work to achieve the things in life that we desire.

MINDSET CHANGES EVERYTHING

Men are slowly forgetting their values and ethics; men these days do not stand up for their self-respect. Women currently hold the majority of power and authority over men, but I still want you to have an ego and self-esteem. Know your worth and never be a simp; always have the mindset that you don't need anybody. You should have the power to leave anyone at any point in their life without feeling anything. Become stoic and eradicate all of your weak emotions. Build a strong, conscious mentality that can combat any kind of evil in this world. Forget about the past and focus on the future.

ALWAYS STRIVE FOR IMPROVEMENT

Progress demands pain; a youngster cannot become a man if he has never experienced hardship, trauma, or stress in his life. A true man is one who overcomes his anxieties and weaknesses You must demonstrate your strength; do not be frail. Don't forget that this world is too harsh for men. Be strong, powerful, and courageous. My one piece of advice to all guys is to never reveal their weaknesses to anyone because you never know who may betray you; sometimes enemies disguise themselves as friends. They cannot attack if they do not know where to attack. Always plan two steps ahead and be cautious in any sort of situation. You should always stay mindful and aware of your surroundings. A guy who strives to improve himself every day, regardless of his existing circumstances, will never fail in life. It takes a lot of indefatigability and persistence to become invincible.

HOW TO BECOME A MAN

Mindset is one of the reasons why a boy is called a man. A 30-year-old man can sometimes be a boy, and a 19-year-old kid can sometimes be a man. If a guy does not know what is vital to him at the moment, he is not a man. A true man never forgets or avoids his responsibilities.

NOTHING HAPPENS BY ACCIDENT

Since society is majorly controlled by the elites (the people above the government who control the world), society encourages men to be weak, feminine, lazy, cowardly, and addicted. We are all puppets to them, so it is critical for a diverse set of people to think differently from the rest of the world. There is a reason why only a few people become successful and wealthy.

If you look around, every man at the top is a true goddamn man. They are not feminine, weak, undisciplined, lazy, or addicted; rather, they are masculine, powerful, disciplined, diligent, and focused. They are radically different from 99 percent of you, which is why they are in the top 1%. They purposely did all of these things because weakening men and oversexualizing society are the first steps towards breaking civilization. Do you think that the wealthy spend their free time watching movies, porn, or TV shows? The entire purpose of subscription services, OTT platforms, and adult sites is to allow you to waste your time viewing worthless content for years and years while remaining unaware of how quickly the time is passing. Can you fathom being so stupid that someone would deliberately take away your time while also making billions from it?

TAKING A REST IS WHAT LOSERS DO

Now you're going to suggest that it's acceptable for a man to occasionally take a break and have fun. I'm sorry, but not until you have attained a particular position or produced a particular value. There are a lot of fantastic things waiting for you in the future; therefore, you must absolutely succeed in living your dream life. Make a circle of individuals around you who are eager to be successful and great in life. I don't see how you can waste your time with people who aren't helping you level up.

Do not waste your time on women who will not add value to your life. Every woman is a distraction, except your wife. Remove any distractions in your life that are restricting your progress. How can you waste your time watching TV and playing video games when you aren't even successful yet?

BE A UNIQUE BREED OF MEN

Don't you ever think that your time for acting like an immature child is over? Kill the boy within yourself and become a mature man. How can you sit on your couch like a slacker, knowing that your family needs you? Grow up, boy, be a man, and break the mental trap that has been ingrained in you for years. The modern world is doing everything it can to make men cowardly and weak.

In this corrupted society, be a unique and different breed of man. You should understand that you must do things that 99 percent of people do not do. The fact of being a guy is that you must have control over your emotions. While some may argue that it is OK to weep, I disagree. It does not imply that I am against a man crying. I understand that there are moments in life when you feel like crying, but I highly advise you not to cry in front of anyone. A man should never expose his vulnerability because you never know who is your enemy and who is your friend. The world is a cruel place, and you must accept that regardless of how kind you believe it is. You need to have a disciplined mindset.

YOUR NOT GIVE A F*CK VERSION EXISTS

A man's potential is determined by how much self-control and stress tolerance he has. A man should do what he is supposed to do, not what he feels like doing. You should know how much emotion to exhibit depending on the scenario; what to show and where to show are two skills you should master within yourself. You should have no interest in how you feel as a man. Even if you are depressed, it should not affect how you act or what you do. There is a version of you who can feel things and still not give a damn about how they make you feel. To become "the man," one must put in a lot of blood and sweat.

WITH GREAT POWER COMES GREAT RESPONSIBILITY

If you want to be "the man," you must also find a trustworthy woman who will push you to improve and become a successful individual.

Find a woman who will always support and understand you—a woman who will become your strength rather than your weakness. There is nothing shameful about having a traditional wife who submits to you and looks towards you as her provider and protector, but with that authority come great responsibilities. Being a man requires a great deal of discipline and stoicism. A man should be a stoic (a person who can withstand pain or suffering without expressing emotion or complaining); you must be physically and emotionally strong. Be courageous; do not express or whine about your problems in life. This world is a battleground, and you are alone in it. You should give your all every day in order to survive.

TEMPORARY PAIN OR ETERNAL SUFFERING

The choice is yours: either have good friends or bad ones; either watch TV or read a book; either play video games or workout; either watch porn or stay focused. Your future will be determined by the path you choose today. You have the option of choosing pleasure today and suffering constantly in the future, or you can choose pain today and experience everlasting happiness in the future. Pain and suffering are extremely vital for a man. A man becomes strong because of all the challenges and hardships he encounters in life. A man who views obstacles positively and overcomes them is a man who succeeds in life. It is entirely up to you whether you use trauma and stress positively or negatively. I advise every man to use it as their ultimate motivator to keep going until they succeed.

IT IS NOT THAT EASY

You have a lot of duties and responsibilities on your shoulder to complete as a man on this earth. You must forego all forms of pleasure and comfort in order to become the man your family and the world require. A youngster primarily becomes a man when he recognizes his responsibilities and duties. To achieve greatness in life, it is necessary to eliminate all distractions and negativity. A boy grows into a man when he focuses on himself to improve every day and works hard to provide a better life for his parents and future life partner. You become mature when you realize that money is the most powerful thing in this world.

Being a true guy requires a lot of self-control, self-assurance, determination, and focus. The media and society are doing all they can to make you cowardly and weak, but do not pay attention to them and stay true to your masculine beliefs.

"They want to rule like a king, but only want the responsibility as of a child."

– Dre Drexler

Men nowadays desire authority without responsibility. In today's world, become a man who understands his responsibilities and duties, a man who never runs away from his responsibilities, no matter how horrible the situation can become. It is not simple to become a real gentleman in modern-day life, but if you genuinely recognize what it takes to be a man and how to become a man, nothing can stop you from achieving greatness in life.

TODAY'S PLEASURE = EXPENSE OF FUTURE LIFE

The modern world is making men weaker by constantly encouraging them to look for an easy alternative. The world and society are cultivating a mindset of weakness; they do not want you to experience adversities and pain; instead, they want you to remain weak. They are promoting weakness amongst us: if things do not go as planned, just quit and move on to something else; if your relationship is becoming difficult and you are not getting along with each other, rather than remaining devoted and working together for the survival of the relationship, just move on and find someone new in your life; if you are frustrated with your life by remaining fat and broke, rather than working on yourself and becoming financially independent, just stay as you are.

The world's pleasures may appear pleasant and make you happy today, but don't forget that they come at the expense of your future life. Either you can enjoy the present while sacrificing your future, or you can enjoy the future while sacrificing your present.

GREATNESS IS WAITING FOR YOU

Do not avoid struggles and hardships in your life, since only difficult times make a man tough. To live in the contemporary world, you must become a warrior, since the world is full of enemies for those who choose a unique path. Most guys are unaware of how much greatness they can achieve as men. You should have a fire in yourself to become the most powerful and successful man on the planet. Nobody is preventing you from dreaming big in life; only you are stopping yourself. You have no idea how blessed you are to have a human existence; it is a shame for you as a man to waste it by being an average person.

PAY HOMAGE TO YOUR ANCESTORS

Your forefathers did not survive all the disasters, wars, and pandemics just for you to stay average. Never forget that you have a duty and an obligation to your bloodline; you owe it to your forefathers. You have no idea how many hardships and struggles (the plague, the black death, wars) your forefathers faced to get you. They would be ashamed to see what they have created. Make an effort to become a man that your ancestors will be proud of, so that they can at least feel that their struggles in the past were worthwhile. You owe them a lot; you can't just play video games and joke around. You cannot end your bloodline by just dying as an average person; they went through hell for your existence. You cannot just abandon your responsibilities and escape from them; doing so is extremely disgraceful for a man. You must decide which path to choose; the decision was and will always be yours.

Choose to serve a higher purpose in life; choose to serve the people you love; choose to serve God. In order for your entire generation to be proud of you, you must attain freedom, free yourself from all the bonds of slavery, and transform into the man you have always wanted to be.

YOU ARE HERE FOR A PURPOSE

Why are you continuously yearning for happiness, why do you want to be happy all the time? Our joyful days are over; we had experienced enough happiness as children; now that we are adults, we are here to suffer and endure misery. We must withstand adversity. You all should realize your goal and purpose as soon as possible, before time runs out. You have responsibilities to fulfil; God never sends someone without a cause or purpose. You are alive for a reason; discover what that is. If you are breathing right now, it only means that God has some unfinished business for you. Never forget that you have a mission and a purpose.

"A man's life is destroyed the moment he chooses a girl over his God-given purpose."

4

WHAT IT TAKES TO BE A WOMAN

Women, in my opinion, are God's most beautiful creation. Can you fathom being granted the honor of giving and creating life by God? A woman should consider herself fortunate because God has endowed her with this wonderful life and ability. As a woman, you must recognize your worth and importance, and you must appreciate your beauty and the body that God has given you. As I said earlier, there is a reason why men and women are born differently and have various qualities. Each of us has a unique role in society.

THE WORLD IS CHANGING

Before I go into how and what it takes to become a woman, I'd like to talk about what women used to confront and how society's opinion of it has changed. Historically, we observed that parents did not prioritize the education of their daughters over that of their sons, but this is changing as time passes. Women used to endure many challenges, such as being forced to stay at home, not having equal rights, physical violence, forced marriages, and much more, but this has all changed. There are still some places where it still happens, but for the most part, things have changed. Women now enjoy equal rights with men in all matters and aspects. In today's society, women have the same opportunities and resources as men. Women can now accomplish whatever men can; there are no limitations for women. Now we'll go into detail about what it means to be a woman from my point of view.

DON'T GO AGAINST THE LAW OF NATURE

In today's society, it is widely propagated that women should be entirely masculine and that it is OK to not be feminine. Surprisingly, both men and women support this, but I want you to understand that the term "masculine" is designated for males (masculine means qualities and appearance associated with men). In the same way that a man cannot be feminine, a woman cannot be masculine. The term itself was created for a certain gender; changing the laws of nature is nearly impossible. Why do you refuse to embrace what God has made you for? You should be proud of yourself.

A woman should be feminine, kind, gentle, and possess qualities such as delicacy and modesty. If you lose touch with your feminine side and become fully masculine, your entire existence as a woman is meaningless.

DENY PSEUDO FEMINISM

This media manipulation will not get you far in society. A woman should understand when to be masculine and when to be feminine. The world loves to see a woman be more feminine since it is one of the things that makes her appear more beautiful. A feminine woman will be liked, complimented, and cared for because of the femininity she possesses. I would like to advise all women not to be influenced by social media and not to change themselves just because of some false feminism. Always remember that you are attractive just the way you are; you do not need masculinity. Never lose sight of the fact that there is always room for self-improvement.

Since it is impossible to achieve perfection in life, it is possible to make yourself better every day than what you were yesterday. A woman who is completely masculine and has killed her feminine side can never live a peaceful and happy life since breaking the norms of nature does not ever bring happiness and harmony.

BEING A WOMAN IS QUITE DIFFICULT

First and foremost, all women need to understand that being a true woman requires a lot of maturity, patience, bravery, devotion, and sacrifice. You can either be a hyper-successful woman who feels she doesn't need a man in her life and can reach the age of 50 happily without a family, or you can be a successful woman who supports her man and believes she needs a man and a family to have a secure and happy life. You may argue that there are many successful women out there who manage both things at the same time, but consider that we are talking about the majority here. Every family has to make some difficult choices and decisions in order to create a happy and peaceful family.

SACRIFICE IS NECESSARY

When a husband and wife both have jobs, it naturally has a detrimental effect on their personal lives, resulting in an emotional imbalance. As a result, children do not receive the love, affection, and value that they require during their youth. To establish a peaceful environment in the family, either a man or a woman has to make greater sacrifices in life. There are several examples in society of famous celebrities separating after only a few years of living together. As a result, it has a harmful influence on children's minds. It is quite uncommon for both of these things to be coordinated together, but when they do, the outcomes are spectacular.

WE BOTH NEED EACH OTHER

Do not be fooled by the media, even if you are a successful man or woman; regardless of what anybody says, remember that we both need each other by our sides. You must understand that any female idol who tells you that you don't need a man and that it's okay to be alone is entirely wrong. They also married a man of greater social status because they understand how the world works: a woman always seeks a man who is more successful and wealthier than she is.

Hypergamy is accepted in the majority of parts of the world. If you ask a woman about what type of man she wants, she will always answer, "I want a powerful, masculine, strong, and successful guy," which indicates she wants to be feminine, kind, gentle, stress-free, and protected. I suggest women use their own judgement to choose what is best for them rather than listening to mainstream media. Don't be deceived by the news and social media nonsense; you only have one life; don't allow false advice and your ego to destroy it.

KNOW WHAT IS BEST FOR YOU

We need more women who understand their roles and responsibilities. I am not opposed to any of the women working, but I am actually proud of the women who are becoming more successful in life and demonstrating what true women's empowerment is. Always do things that make you happy in life; the option is yours to determine the type of life you desire. It is up to you and your partner to manage your relationship and guide your family towards happiness. Because western culture is not widely established in India, I want to warn all women and men not to be influenced by this wave of pseudo-feminism and so-called toxic masculinity.

WHAT TRANSFORMS A GIRL INTO A WOMAN

A girl becomes a woman when she realizes she has to quit all the parties, focus on herself, get highly educated, learn about values, become successful in life, and be prepared to be a loyal, supportive, and caring woman for her future spouse and family. Stop spending time hanging out with your friends, going to bars, complaining about each other, and sleeping with guys that don't even deserve you. Find your life's purpose and strive persistently to achieve it. You don't have enough time to prove your worth. Life is not fair to people who sit around making excuses. A man is looked into his future to see if he will be able to provide for and protect his family, as well as how successful and wealthy he will be in the future, whereas a woman is looked into her past to see what she was, how educated she is, what she faced previously, whether her life was traumatic, and if she is caring and loving.

PROVE YOUR WORTH

Make yourself a woman your spouse and family can be proud of. It takes a lot of sacrifices to become a woman who leads the world and society towards prosperity. The world needs women who are aware of their value and worth. a woman who is independent, fearless, bold, and capable of standing up for her rights. No matter how bad the situation becomes, a woman should never attempt to escape her responsibilities. Never lose sight of why you are living; show the world who you are and what you are capable of. You must realize that there is discrimination in this world.

A guy will not be criticized for having several relationships with women, but a woman will be criticized for having multiple relationships with men.

You must realize that the world is unfair and that changing society's mindset is very challenging, but it is up to you to figure out how to prove to the rest of the world that you are a woman of value. Make every effort to develop into a woman who is self-assured, self-reliant, successful, kind, gentle, loyal, and understanding. A good woman is driven by self-determined values, has high self-worth yet is down-to-earth, and demonstrates strength, bravery, and compassion. Be the kind of lady your children will be proud to represent as their mother in the future. There is a time when it is OK to act and behave like a girl, but eventually you must realize that you must become a woman, and it is better if you do it as soon as possible.

HARD TO LIVE OUT THERE

Women frequently encounter several issues in their daily lives. A woman's life is also not simple; she is judged on a variety of subjects, harassed in various ways on a daily basis, and restricted in multiple ways. Even today, women are harassed, sexually molested, attacked, and discriminated against unfairly in many parts of our countries. Women commonly suffer from a variety of issues, including anxiety, sadness, and other disorders. In the same way that men need a woman in their lives, women should also realize that they need a guy as well. Again, I'm attempting to shed light on the fact that you should never blindly trust the news or social media lies; if you dive deep enough into these topics, you will discover a very dark truth lurking beneath the surface. In my opinion, it is a woman's responsibility to care for her husband, provide serenity in his life, care for her children, and maintain harmony in the family.

Understanding these responsibilities requires a huge amount of discipline, sacrifice, and maturity. I never advise women to be influenced by what other people say, but unfortunately, we are all striving for respect and prestige in society.

YOUR FEMININTY IS BEAUTIFUL IN ITSELF

You will be admired and accepted as a woman only if you have female qualities and attributes. A feminine woman will always be valued more than a hyper masculine woman. When a woman is feminine, she looks more lovely and is more valued. A woman's beauty lies in her femininity. A woman should be aware of when she should be masculine and when she should be feminine. A man is referred to as a man because of his masculine side, while a woman is referred to as a woman because of her feminine side. There is a reason why God alone gave women this magnificent ability and power to create life. Women are considerably better than men in terms of child care and nurturing.

YOU HAVE A DUTY TO BE A TRUE WOMAN

Men expect women to be strong at times, and it is a woman's responsibility to recognize when this is required. In the same way that it is a man's responsibility to provide for and protect his wife and family, it is a woman's responsibility to spiritually protect and care for her husband while also providing peace and love to the family. You can switch roles, but most of the time it does not come with positive results. Empathy, compassion, resilience, caring, cooperation, and self-care are some traits and attributes that make a woman more beautiful. A woman should be empathic and have the capacity to connect with and understand each other on an emotional level. Women play an essential role in providing love and compassion to society as a whole. God has given women the capacity to heal spiritually. Compassion and concern for another person demonstrate that she is emotionally linked to her feelings, which is a huge indicator of a true woman. Women play an integral role in society.

FOUNDATION OF FAMILY

The central place of women in society has always safeguarded a country's stability, advancement, and long-term growth. They serve as the foundation of families and are essential to the growth and development of communities. A woman should be resilient; resilience is the capacity to recover from and overcome adversity in life. A true woman always remains strong in any scenario; she should be capable of dealing with challenges in her life while adapting to changes in attributes linked with femininity.

> *"The world needs strong women. Women who will lift and build others, who will love and be loved. Women who live bravely, both tender and fierce. Women of indomitable will."*
>
> *– Amy Tenny*

Being a woman involves having a stronger sense of identity, accepting your body as one that changes and evolves through time, being self-assured, and uplifting others around you. It means you have the wisdom to be grateful for what you have while still being hungry for growth. A woman should be aware of when she must make sacrifices in her life for the sake of herself and her family. She should understand what is vital for her right now and what will lead her to a better and happier future. A woman's life is full of judgement and pressure; you must ignore the perspective of others if you want to grow and develop personally.

HOW TO BECOME A WOMAN

There are certain fundamental factors that distinguish a girl from a woman. As I previously stated, there can be a 31-year-old mature woman who is still a girl and a 19-year-old small girl who is now a woman. It all comes down to how you think, how your brain works, and how mature you are.

CREATE YOUR VALUE

It is incorrect to assume that maturity comes with age; rather, maturity comes from the events and issues you have faced throughout your life. Incidents and suffering shape a person. To be a woman, you must be compassionate, kind, strong, bold, understanding, and mature. It requires a lot of commitment, sacrifices, compassion, empathy, cooperation, management, and understanding to adapt these qualities. Nobody can become perfect, but you can try your hardest to change your flaws one by one and become a better version of yourself every day. The world and society want to ruin your inner beauty and turn you into a girl with no worth or respect in the future. Reject all traps set by those who are degrading your value in your eyes and in society. Don't make yourself available to someone who doesn't respect your time. You are the only one who can determine your own worth.

Choose a man who can add value to your life, who is ambitious, has future goals, and is committed to living a successful life. Choosing an appropriate partner for yourself is vital because you will behave the way he acts and live the way he lives. It is a natural tendency for a woman to follow her husband's guidance. If the man is not serious about progressing in life and is not attempting to make his family's life better, it will naturally influence the woman's life.

BECOME THE GREATEST

You must comprehend what your life's purpose is and what you desire from it. Your decisions in life will determine how you will live your life and how you'll be recognized as a person and a woman. There are several examples of great women in India, including Rani Laxmi Bai, Kalpana Chawla, Mary Kom, Saina Nehwal, Arunima Sinha, Mithali Raj, and many others. We need women who can be strong and bold with their emotions and who can become fearless when the situation calls for it. If you gaze closely in the mirror at yourself, you will realize your own worth and the truth about yourself. If you don't feel proud of yourself when you look in the mirror, it's time to make a change in your life.

We are all here to suffer and grow every day. With time, you'll realize what you need to do in life. The shift from girlhood to womanhood is associated with some qualities.

GIRLHOOD TO WOMANHOOD

The development of emotional and intellectual maturity helps a girl transform from a girl to a woman. It involves many things, including accepting responsibility for one's actions, making sincere and significant decisions, and having a sense of self-awareness to distinguish between good and bad people. In fact, it is believed that women have an extra sense that enables them to decipher a person's intentions for them. Gaining a sense of independence and autonomy is a necessary part of becoming a woman; this may be accomplished in a variety of ways, including being financially independent, making autonomous decisions, and developing a strong sense of self.

Women are generally expected to have higher emotional intelligence, including compassion and empathy. It involves understanding and managing one's emotions as well as having a soft side. It is a woman's responsibility to maintain peace in society. Self-confidence is essential in transitioning from a girl to a woman. a higher feeling of self-confidence, which involves believing in one's own skills and being at ease with one's own body.

THE JOURNEY IS MAGNIFICENT

Empowerment in oneself can take many forms, including greater education, following one's goals and desires, and trying to make the world a better place to live. Resilience is one of the finest attributes a woman can have. If you are resilient, mental health conditions such as depression and anxiety may be less likely to affect you. Bullying and trauma are two factors that resilience can help to counteract. Understanding and accepting reality while continuing to accomplish what is necessary is a tremendous quality that every woman should cultivate. Growing from a girl to a woman, becoming educated, working a job or starting her own business, getting married, having children, and having a lovely family is a beautiful journey. It is not easy to become a true lady, but it is also not that tough if you understand what it takes.

It is also about time, age, comprehension, priorities, and decisions. You should constantly be aware of the obligations and responsibilities that you are carrying on your shoulders. A true woman never escapes her obligations and responsibilities.

"A strong woman knows she has strength enough for the journey, but a woman of strength knows it is in the journey where she will become strong."

– Luke Easter

5

IT IS EASIER FOR WOMEN THAN MEN IN MODERN WORLD

The world is a cruel and harsh place to live. Not just men, but also women, must be tough and powerful. It is not easy for any of us to survive; thus, we must strive to be the best versions of ourselves. It's all about "survival of the fittest." It signifies that the one who is consistent, disciplined, diligent, focused, and gives their hardest regardless of how they feel can only win in this world. In this world, there is a large population that is in need. Every person in the modern world faces issues and obstacles in their daily lives.

LET'S EXPOSE THE REALITY

Both men and women have various issues and struggles throughout their lives; however, in this article, I will thoroughly explain to all of the readers why women's lives are simpler than men's by providing some additional context. It doesn't mean that I'm arguing that women's lives aren't difficult or that they don't encounter issues; rather, I'm stating that in the modern world, women have it easier than men. Now, for all the women who are assuming that it can't possibly be real, I will advise you to read the entire topic first before deciding what is correct and what is wrong. In this article, I will show you all the reality of men's lives with instances from your daily experience. Truth will remain truth regardless of whether someone accepts it or not.

"Truth is not something outside to be discovered, it is something inside to be realized."

– Osho

STANDARDS WORK DIFFERENTLY

Let us start with the differences in standards between men and women. Society would not criticize a woman who says, "I want a man who is taller than me, stronger than me, earns more money than me, is more intellectual and mature than me, is more successful than me, and is gorgeous." Everyone will try to convince you that every woman has the right to find a man who is better than her. However, if a guy says, "I don't want a short woman, I don't want a woman who earns less than me, I don't want a woman who is weak, I don't want a fat woman, and I don't want an unattractive woman," society will criticize him and say, "How can you ask for these things?" He will be labelled a weirdo for passing judgement on a lady and humiliated for expressing his thoughts.

Men's standards are criticized, whereas women's standards are praised. In today's modern environment, a woman's standards are significantly more unrealistic than a man's. Let me ask you all a question. Is it difficult to increase height or reduce weight? without a doubt! It is tough to grow in height. So, does this not demonstrate that beauty standards are harder for young men as compared to young women?

UNBELIEVABLY TOUGH

A man is expected to bring far more to the table than a woman. The majority of women choose a tall, powerful, handsome, wealthy, humorous, and charming man, while men just want a loyal and beautiful lady. It is significantly more difficult for guys since women have unrealistic expectations while men live in reality. Life is very difficult for men; a man cannot openly share his opinions on women in public on the internet because he is afraid of being charged for any hateful speech or comment; a man does not have the freedom to put his views out there, and if he does, he will be considered a low-value man with old-school thoughts; but a woman can openly share her opinions on men without hesitation because she has the privilege and freedom to say anything on the internet without fear.

WHAT TO DO YOU WANT?

It is difficult for a male to comprehend women since they rarely articulate what they truly feel and are not honest about their emotions. It is a lot difficult for a man to understand women because most of the times they don't say what they really feel and they are not true about their feelings. Sometimes, women say one thing and do it's opposite. A woman says, "I want a man who is powerful, strong, and has emotional control over his feelings," but they also say, "Why don't you show your feelings and tell how you feel?" When a man shows his true internal feelings, women begin to lose feelings for him and begin to see him as an incapable and weak man. It has been seen several times that women lose affection for their boyfriends when he weeps or displays his weak side to them. A guy has no choice since he will be criticized in both ways, whether he expresses his emotions or not.

Therefore, the best advice I can provide to all guys is to be stoic, disciplined, and have emotional control over themselves, because no one likes a weak man, no matter what anyone says. Every mother wants a strong son, every daughter wants a strong father, every sister wants a strong brother, and every woman wants a strong husband. Your only option as a guy is to be strong.

When a man has an opinion on the type of woman he desires, his viewpoint is frequently criticized and not supported, but a woman's viewpoint is supported by both men on women. Nobody judges a woman for having preferences about the type of man she desires. To put it another way, "a man will be judged for his opinions, but a woman will not."

"MEN'S MENTAL HEALTH MATTERS" IS A LIE

Let us now go on to the next topic: no one cares about a man's feelings. A man who expresses his feelings frequently is a weak man in my opinion, since as a man, you must compete with other men in every part of life —physical, mental, and emotional. One of the worst mistakes a man makes is showing or telling someone his weakness. However, in this topic, I will show and explain that a man's sentiments and emotions don't matter to the world, and no one cares about them. A woman's sentiments are always recognized and accepted by society; no one condemns a woman for expressing how she truly feels, but a guy's feelings have never mattered to anybody, and no one cares about how a man feels.

The media is always misleading you; try to understand that no one cares about men's mental health. Every year, the number of men who commit suicide increases. If men are committing suicide at an increasing rate, does this not demonstrate that no one cares about men's mental health, since if men were treated with love and care, suicide rates would have declined each year? The world pretends to care about it, but only a guy knows the truth. No one cares what you are going through if you are a man.

PERSPECTIVE DIFFERENCE WITHIN THE WORLD

Let me give you an example: if a woman cries in public, everyone rushes over to check on her. Everyone will be concerned about her—are you okay? Is everything fine? Is everything all right with you? No one will pass judgement on her, laugh at her, or neglect her. She will be treated like a VIP and asked for everything necessary until she stops sobbing, but if a man cries in public, no one will care about him, and everyone will completely ignore him as if he does not exist. No one will help him or perhaps even ask what the problem is, instead mocking and criticizing him. No one will even consider the possibility that he is suffering from something terrible in his life or that he requires some love, affection, and care in his life.

A guy should not be allowed to overly express his sentiments because a man who lacks control over his feelings and emotions is a weak man, and the world does not tolerate weak men. Women believe that men should express their feelings more openly, but they are unaware of what will happen if men get extremely emotional and lose control of themselves.

MEN WITHOUT EMOTIONAL CONTROL ARE DANGEROUS

The most dangerous person on the planet is an emotional man. Behind all of the crimes, murders, murders, and rapes are guys who lack emotional control. Men with a sense of control and understanding know the importance of having control over their bodies and words. A man should not express his true feelings since doing so reveals your flaws, and men have never been praised for displaying their weakness since the dawn of time; hence, it is vital for a man to become stoic, disciplined, and masculine. A guy has just one option: destroy the sentiments that make him weak, because exhibiting emotions is bad for man and always results in negative consequences and outcomes.

It is in a woman's instinct to rebel against it, since if a man cries in front of her, a visceral switch in her head signals her that this person cannot protect and provide for her. It doesn't matter if it's just a moment of weakness; weakness is weakness for a woman.

YOU ARE ALONE, MAN!

As a result, a man's sole alternative is to convey his feelings to himself. One should know when and where to express his feelings. In our contemporary society, a woman can never feel lonely since she can always find someone to understand and listen to her, but for a man, finding someone by his side is much more difficult, and most of them stay entirely alone the entire time. Women have no idea how lonely the majority of men are nowadays. There are plenty of men out there who are genuinely lonely. Can you imagine how your life would be if you couldn't discuss or express your feelings and thoughts to anyone, but yourself? The reality is that the majority of a man's life is depressing and stressful. There has been data research that demonstrates that men's suicidal rate is four times higher than women's on average, so does this not reflect that who is suffering the most and who has a difficult life?

NO ONE CARES

In today's cultural world, a man's anxiety, stress, sadness, and depression are regarded as a joke, and no one takes them seriously, whereas a woman's anxiety, stress, sorrow, and depression are always treated seriously, given significance, and are not judged by anyone. The events and problems that men confront are very different from those that women experience. Do not misunderstand me to believe that I am anti-women; I agree that women's lives are difficult and that women face a variety of challenges, but I am arguing the fact that it is more difficult for men than women, as I demonstrated above, and I want to discuss it further because the struggle does not end here.

DIVORCES ARE KILLING THE SOCIETY

Women have no idea how difficult it is for men to exist in today's environment. According to the ASA (American Sociological Association), women initiate divorce 70 percent of the time, and the scale reaches 90 percent when it comes to college-educated women. I understand that this is a Western issue, but its influence has a significant impact on us as well. Don't you think how difficult it is for a man to be left by a person to whom he has given his entire life, love, care, and affection, and then everything shatters in a matter of seconds. Can you imagine how painful it is for a guy to see his family disintegrate into pieces for which he has worked his entire life? Divorce is prevalent in the West, and it is already affecting India. We can observe the shift in metropolises where modernism is at its peak, and one day our condition will be similar to that of the West. You don't comprehend, but it will be far worse than your worst nightmare.

I addressed it before, but I felt it would be beneficial to highlight that a large majority of individuals claim they have never been caught having an affair (81 percent men and 92 percent women). Even if some of them were discovered, the findings did not result in divorce for 77 percent of men and 62 percent of women. Just because there aren't many divorces in India doesn't imply our society is advancing. There are several more factors in India that prevent people from making this decision.

WOMEN (BORN WITH VALUE UP TO SOME LEVEL) = MEN (CREATE VALUE)

I don't understand why the world refuses to accept the truth, even when it is there in front of their faces. Women are born with intrinsic worth, while men have to develop their own. Women will be respected, loved, cared for, and treated properly without condition, as can be seen all across the world. Women are born with value; they do not need to manufacture their own because they know society will accept them for who they are and what they are. They are not subjected to societal pressure, stress, or force to be something or someone (in essence, they have an alternative option), but men are not born with any value; it is necessary and mandatory for them to create their own value because society does not accept a man who lacks any value or status.

Only under certain conditions would a man be respected, loved, cared for, and treated nicely. If you are a useless man, you will witness how cold and brutal the world is; no one cares about you at all. In other words, women are loved unconditionally, but a man will only be loved under certain conditions.

> *"There is no other way for a man to become valuable than by going through suffering and pain."*
>
> *– Aditya Gupta*

WOMEN'S LIVES ARE MUCH MORE VALUABLE THAN MEN'S LIVES.

Man has no other choice but to create worth in order to be respected and loved. Women are born with innate value; they will always be significant because they can reproduce and generate life, but a man's status is determined only by how valuable and useful he is. Let me give you an example: Even If a woman is not attractive, intelligent, or at a particular level, she will still receive attention, affection, love, and respect; while, a man will only receive attention, affection, love, and respect if he is handsome, brave, has reached a certain level, earns well, and has some value in society. Women are born with all of these privileges, but men have to work for them. Women often ignore the fact that men are born with zero intrinsic value. If 100 men died anywhere, it would not be a huge concern or an issue; however, if 100 women died elsewhere, it would be a big deal since women's lives are far more valued and precious than men's lives. You are significant and useful to the world and society.

EXPECTED TO BRING FAR MORE THINGS ON TABLE

A woman will not accept a man as her spouse until he protects and provides for her. You will be respected and loved based on how valuable you are to society. Men are held to higher standards than women; They are expected to bring far more to the table than women in order to be liked and respected. Society has much higher expectations of men in every aspect of life; it is more difficult for guys out there. A man must do things regardless of how he feels, whether he is pleased or unhappy. A man cannot relax since no one will come to rescue him, while a woman can relax while still attracting a high-status man. Women can quit their jobs and remain at home whenever they choose, but men cannot.

MODERN WOMEN ARE FAR MORE DELUSIONAL

Men love women for who they are, while women love men for who they will become. Men truly love women because when a guy loves a woman, he accepts her as she is and does not want anything from her, however when a woman loves a man, she expects him to change himself for her. Men love women idealistically, while women love men opportunistically. Women are significantly more delusory about love, and it is not their fault. From a young age, girls are taught ridiculous fairy tales about how one day a prince on a horse will come and carry you away with him. They are taught that they are the prize and that in spite of their lack of work, they deserve everything. They have been groomed with false expectations since infancy, but there comes a point in her life when she discovers how she has been deceived the entire time. The media and society have both contributed to the development of a delusory worldview.

LOVE WORKS DIFFERENTLY

Men's and women's love is completely different. Studies show that women take longer to fall in love than men do. A woman takes considerably longer to conclude that he is the one, while a man usually chooses within a short period of time since men fall in love with what they see.

If a man loves a woman, he doesn't care what her status is, how much she earns, how beautiful she is, or what the rest of the world thinks about her. But when a woman loves a man, she considers everything before falling in love with him, including his status, how much money he earns, whether he is ambitious or not, and whether he can protect me or not. Women can fall in love without evaluating a guy, but the outcomes are not often credible. As previously said, men are loved conditionally, whereas women are loved unconditionally.

There is a reason why heartbreaks are harder for men than for women. For a man, losing a woman is similar to losing a child because you protect and care for her, whereas for a woman, losing a man is similar to losing a parent, and we are evolutionarily psychologically crafted to deal with losing parents better than we are with losing children.

IT IS EASY TO SAY MEN ARE IN PRIVILEGE

According to research, men suffer much more than women through heartbreak, and in the worst situations, this results in violence. A woman will receive sympathy, affection, care, and understanding during a breakup; a guy will not receive any of these things. No one will understand his grief and emotions, and he will suffer alone all of the time. A woman can quickly find another guy to provide her with comfort and relief, but a man cannot. A woman cannot comprehend how depressing a man's life can be. It is extremely difficult to exist as a guy if you lack value, position, and money. A man is worthless in this world if he is not useful. If you think about it, most men have it tough out there. Humans require love, affection, and care in order to live a happy and positive existence. It is far easier for women to find love, affection, and caring than it is for men. Even if you are an ugly, overweight, dull, or immature woman, you will still draw attention, but an ordinary, ugly, and fat guy would be invisible.

BEING ORDINARY IS NOT AN OPTION

Most guys do not receive attention, love, or affection throughout their lives. These things will be available to you as a man only after you reach a certain level. A man must battle and struggle throughout his life for love, affection, and attention, but women receive all of these things from the moment they are born. To gain love, affection, and attention, you simply need to be a girl or a woman. You can be an average woman and yet grab attention, whereas 99 percent of men will go to a club and not get any. The majority of men are absolutely invisible, and social media has played a significant role in this. This modern world is all about show-offs and fame. You will see each and every female getting hundreds of follow requests and guys sliding into her DMs.

Most of the girls have alternatives to select a person of their choice, but if you are an ordinary man, no one cares. You will be neglected by everyone, and your presence will be meaningless in the social world and even in actual life.

THINGS DON'T WORK THE SAME WAY

A man working in a restaurant, café, or hotel is utterly invisible in today's society. No woman would ever consider dating a guy like him, but if the genders are reversed, the situation is completely different. There are many women who work in a restaurant, café, or hotel who have no value or position but yet date well-established and wealthy men just because they are attractive. A rich man dating an ordinary woman is possible, but a rich woman dating an average man is not. Isn't it unjust? Yes, it is, but we have no control over it. Hence, a man has no choice but to become valuable. Most men do not have the same options that women do in their lives.

The majority of guys do not have even one woman by their side to encourage and respect them. Men suffer from loneliness, sadness, anxiety, and other problems as a result of this. This world is a harsh place for men who have no worth. To be respected and liked, you must be important.

"If a man favours men over women, this does not imply that he despises women or is a misogynist. Many men out there assist the male community more than the female community while still having a wonderful and pleasant life with their families."

Women believe that men have everything: power, money, control, and so on, but they don't realize that they are talking about men in the top ten percent; 90 percent of men do not have money, power, or control. They don't have any joy or happiness in their lives; they only suffer alone in the dark. Women mix 90 percent of men with the top ten percent of men.

WE CAN'T AVOID IT

Men have to provide and protect; they cannot avoid their responsibilities. A guy has no choice but to suffer; no one will come to save you; you are on your own in this world. For example, if a man and a woman are walking down the street late at night and a bunch of men assault the lady, the guy has no choice but to fight them at the risk of his life. It makes no difference what kind of connection he has with her or how important she is to him. He has to put his life in danger in order to defend the woman. It is his responsibility as a man, and he cannot avoid it; but those who avoid their duties are weak individuals who deserve nothing in this life. Do you realize that the majority of men are victims of homicides, the majority of men are victims of violent crimes, and men receive longer sentences for the same crime than women, but you still think it is simpler for men? Women are born with an innate privilege that men do not have. So we'll discuss it more in our next topic, "Who is in Privilege?"

6

WHO IS IN PRIVILEGE?

The modern world has evolved dramatically in recent years, and you do not need to comprehend it through theory or book reading. You can readily see how society and the world have evolved in every aspect. The world has advanced, and it is no longer the ancient days. People's minds have been brainwashed into believing that men have a privilege. Before we get started, let me define privilege. It is a special advantage, right, or opportunity that is provided to a certain individual or group of people. It is caused by societal or structural variables such as money, status, gender, race, and so on. In simple words, it is an advantage and a positive factor in the world in several ways. So, do you believe that men have privileges over women in today's modern world?

The nonsense that social media, news, and elite manipulators have embedded in your mind is difficult to remove, but if you have even a smidgeon of understanding of your own decision-making power and mind, you will understand the reality behind all of the truth and the blind show that everyone is putting on for you.

THINGS ARE NOT THE SAME AS THEY WERE IN THE PAST

In the past, men would go to work and earn money for their homes and families, while women would perform housework, care for children, cook for the family, and maintain peace and happiness at home. Women were physically assaulted in the past and did not have the same rights, opportunities, facilities, or resources as men. Men used to have greater power in the past. Throughout history, men have occupied positions of leadership, had better access to education, and had larger chances for political, economic, and social participation. Women were mostly assigned household and caregiving responsibilities. They suffered a variety of legal and cultural constraints, including a lack of voting rights and limited authority over property. These inequities and discrimination against women have existed for a long time.

Slowly, as time passed, the world evolved and started to take these things seriously, and due to this, things began to change. The rights have been in the constitution since the past, and some were later implemented, but everything changed gradually through time. Now we live in the 21st century —a new era, a new period of time in which everything has changed, not only in terms of men and women but also in terms of technology, education, culture, livelihood, and many other things.

FEMINISM > PSEUDO FEMINISM

In the past, men had power, money, knowledge, and rights, but things have changed. Feminism has played a significant role in assisting women to gain equal rights and opportunities in the world, and it is good on certain levels. However, in today's time, not only women, but also men continue to accept the poison of fake feminism. A feminist is someone who believes that women should have the same rights and opportunities as men. They currently have equality, but if you seek oppression and wish to suppress men, then it is practically a sort of fake feminism. Since 1996, pseudo feminism, or fake feminism, has taken over nations such as India. Politicians, anti-national elements, state-sponsored terrorists, and even liberals have all played a role in the creation of fake-feminism or pseudo-feminism, which was also done on purpose to weaken society and men so that elites can easily govern and apply their rules and regulations, which are not always in the best interests of society; you can call it a "blind play." It is simply an illusion to demonstrate that something is done for your benefit and advantage while they benefit indirectly from that activity through several sources. The entire objective of discussing it was to demonstrate who is truly privileged, and we will discuss several cases to reveal the actual reality.

YOUR LIFE HAS VALUE

Women believe that men have easy lives, but they do not realize that a man's sentiments and existence are not valued by anybody; they just suffer all the time without being acknowledged by the world. As I previously stated, if 100 men die in an accident, no one will care, but if 100 women die, it will be a big deal. You are a life creator, and your presence is far more vital to the planet than men's. Women's lives were valued not just today, but also in the past. Take the Titanic incident as an example. At first, only the women and children were saved and placed in the lifeboat; do you think they didn't want to go first? Of course they did, since they knew it was the man's responsibility to put his family first. "Was it a privilege to be a man in such a situation?"

You must understand that most men suffer every day of their lives and have no control over it. There may have been privilege in the past, but there is none in today's modern society. If you are successful and in the top 10 %, you will have a huge amount of privilege; most men do not reach that level, so it is all about the majority.

BRAINWASHING IS WORKING

Women nowadays don't even respect their men because of the fake feminism nonsense and garbage that the media has instilled in their heads. Men must attain a specific level or acquire a certain amount of money and prestige in order to be respected not just in society but also in their families. If a father does not earn money and is unable to meet the needs of his children and wife, one day his children and even his wife will say to him, "What have you done for us?" "You are not capable of fulfilling our wishes," "Work hard to earn more money," "You are not worthy of anything," even if he is giving 100 percent to his work and trying his hardest. The world is cruel, so consider twice before telling a man that it is a privilege to be a man. Man cannot survive in the modern world without status and respect.

WE ARE TOTALLY DIFFERENT

On average, men commit suicide four times more than women each year, and the numbers are rising. Even in the past, it was not a luxury to be a man if certain things were overlooked. When there was a war in the past and the country was short on military personnel, all the men and even boys were compelled to fight for their country without their consent, and this even occurs in certain countries today. As an example, during the Russia-Ukraine war, no man or boy above the age of 18 is permitted to leave the nation, and specific requirements must be met for a man to exit the country.

We'll look at a few cases and have a full discussion on privilege. We'll use a few cases to have a more in-depth discussion on privilege.

WOMEN ARE BORN WITH AN INNATE VALUE

Let's imagine a woman is travelling by train; she is standing with luggage and has no seat reservation. I bet you that she will be invited to sit down and will have enough space to complete the journey. Whereas if it were a man, no one would care, no one would help him, no one would even give him a little space, and he would spend the entire journey standing in the train or sitting on the floor. "Is it a privilege to be a man?"

NOBODY UNDERSTAND MEN

A man cannot talk to anyone about his stress, anxiety, and sadness, not even his parents, because in his parents' eyes he is a grown strong man, and even if he shares his feelings with his friends, most of his friends will laugh at him for acting like a child, and even if he tells his girlfriend or wife, he will look weak, and they will no longer respect him; society will judge him and taunt him. Thus, a man has to face everything alone most of the time and suffer in his mind like hell, whereas if a woman is depressed, anxious, or stressed, she can talk to anyone and has countless options; she doesn't have to imagine how others will perceive her or how society will judge her; it is as simple as that, no pressure. She will receive compassion, love, care, emotional support, and someone to express her thoughts with; no one will laugh at her or make fun of her; and her parents will take it seriously and help her overcome it till she is fine. Everyone will try to comprehend a woman's condition, but what about men? "Is it a privilege to be a man?"

This is how society and the world work, and you have no control over it. You can only accept things, go on, and grow stronger each day. Being unemployed and destitute is akin to being a garbage can (useless).

BORN CONDITIONAL

I've already stated it, but I'd like to bring it up again. As humans, we desire love, compassion, and respect. Women are loved unconditionally; they are cherished, cared for, and valued without expecting anything in return. Most women are respected without being asked; they get attention throughout their lives, especially when they are young. They receive what they want without even asking for it. Getting complimented and appreciated is not uncommon in today's culture for women, but it is the absolute opposite for men. They are not loved, cared for, or respected until they have a particular position, money, value, and power, and they are only loved if they ask for attention, care, and affection and even beg for it most of the time. They survive without physical love and sex, but if a female wants it, she can get it at any time with only a phone call or text. They have hundreds of guys begging for their attention and affection on social media. What they need to do is pick up one guy and message "Hi." It's as simple as that for them.

THE WORLD'S MAJORITY OF MEN JUST SUFFER

The false narrative in people's minds is undermining their respect for men. People feel that the majority of men are pleasantly enjoying and spending their lives, while the majority of them are broken from the inside. The majority of men do not have authority, and they do have their emotional and physical needs fulfilled and controlled according to women's choices. They cannot say, "I want to have sex today," because he will be criticized and shamed for asking, whereas women can easily ask for physical satisfaction, and her man cannot say no even when he does not want it because she is in control, and if he says no, most of the time, women start ignoring her man, become rude, and stop the men from even touching her, whereas most of the women can go to anyone and easily get it.

ACCORDING TO LAW, MEN CANNOT BE VICTIMS

"You can't force a woman, but a woman can force her man." No court will listen to your complaint or even consider it an issue, and no one will believe that a guy can be assaulted or harassed. Sometimes, many women even make false allegations against their men in order to get rid of them. "Is it a privilege to be a man?" I'm being utterly biased here, but that doesn't mean guys don't have any sort of privilege. In India, there are still certain regions where women are oppressed by men. But in this case, I'm referring to metropolises in India, such as Delhi, Mumbai, and Bangalore, where modernity has gained ground.

TRY TO UNDERSTAND ONE ANOTHER

Western culture has begun to affect India and will spread throughout the country within a few decades (in the majority of regions). I expect that both modern-day girls and women will comprehend how men feel. You may not realize it, but most of them are genuinely damaged on the inside, and they sometimes need a girl or a woman by their side who can just listen to them, understand their pain, provide them some peace and comfort, make them believe in themselves again, and support them in their failures. I also expect guys to comprehend women's emotions and try to fulfil their needs. I'll show you one last example, which is quite severe, and I hope that it changes soon.

WE CANNOT STAND UP FOR OURSELVES

If a woman makes false allegations of sexual harassment, physical assault, or rape against a man, cops will arrest him without any proof. They will throw him in jail without even questioning the person or demanding evidence from the woman. The individual will be behind the locker in a matter of minutes. He will not be able to defend his innocence or present evidence against the woman until he shows up in court. Women can fabricate scars on themselves several times and appear to have been raped if they wish to seek revenge or ruin a man's life. According to the National Crime Records Bureau (NCRB), about 74% of rape cases under Section 376 of the Indian Penal Code end up acquitting the accused. We all think about the women who suffered from it, but what about the men whose lives got ruined just because of some fake allegations? Surprisingly, most men percent of men have no control over the issue.

INNOCENT UNTIL PROVEN GUILTY, GUILTY UNTIL PROVEN INNOCENT

There have been several examples in India where men have been imprisoned for years and years, and later it was discovered that they were innocent. A famous phrase goes, "A man is guilty until proven innocent, while a woman is innocent until proven guilty." However, most of the time, women are still innocent even after being proven guilty. This is the power that women currently have, and it is an example of "misuse of power." There is no severity to the man's case; they cannot fathom that men can be raped, sexually harassed, or physically abused.

Some men are threatened by their wives through false accusations or divorce threats. There are many victims, not just married guys but also youngsters whose girlfriends falsely accused them in order to seek revenge and satisfy their egos. Courts are prejudiced towards women; I hope it changes soon. Courts should listen to both sides or parties, give everyone a fair chance to prove themselves, and then draw conclusions. so that no innocent person gets punished for the crime he did not commit. At last, I am finally asking again, "Is it a privilege to be a man?" I brought this issue up because it is vital to demonstrate to the world that being a man is not an advantage these days.

"Privilege varies from person to person, and both genders have positive and negative aspects in different ways, which I absolutely agree with. But if we take the majority of people

and consider the benefits and drawbacks of both genders in all areas, women, in my opinion, are privileged in today's modern world. This was already discussed in detail in one of my topics, "Why is it easier for women than men in the modern world?"

7

YOU DON'T DESERVE

If I'm correct, you're probably wondering what this topic is about. You will comprehend it if you read it whole; it cannot be stated in just a few words. This world is full of complaints, lethargy, regret, fraud, and excuses. Most people want to appear better, work harder, become rich, successful, knowledgeable, famous, powerful, and so on, but they don't want to work for it. Let me ask you all one question: Does anyone force you to do anything? Are you a slave to anyone? Is someone limiting your progress? No, right! Then why don't you get out of bed and work for what you want? It could be anything: you want to be wealthy, fit, and muscular; you want to have a girlfriend or boyfriend; you want to be respected; you want to travel the world; you want to purchase your dream automobile; or you want to make your parents proud.

NO ONE IS COMING TO SAVE YOU

You desire it from the bottom of your heart, and anytime you see someone else get it, you become sad or regret it. But you scumbags don't grasp a basic goddamn thing that they worked their asses off to acquire what they desired. No one is coming to help you; no one is going to give you a Ferrari to drive; no one is going to give you millions of dollars of cash to live your dream lifestyle; no one is going to pay your bills; no one is going to give you a hot girlfriend or boyfriend; no one is going to take you to the gym and make you fit. Only you have the ability to change it. The world is a pretty rough place to exist, and if you are not striving to improve yourself on a daily basis or working hard, you should prepare yourself for endless suffering. If someone else in the world is working harder than you for the same thing, how can you blame God for not providing you with what you desire?

God appreciates individuals who make an effort and work hard. God provides success to those who truly desire it. The one who deserves it receives it.

WORLD IS A BATTLE GROUND

This world is about player versus player; it is a battleground, and everyone is trying their hardest to survive here. However, life is about living, not surviving. Everyone is writing their own tale, and only a handful will emerge victorious. You may decide whether you want to live your life as a winner or a loser. If you want to live the best life possible, you must be prepared for the worst-case scenario. You have to pay the price for everything because life is about giving with one hand and taking with the other. In essence, most individuals create excuses for their lives, saying things such as, "I deserve that," "I worked more than him/her," and "I am better than him/her." I'm sorry for being cruel, but if you had deserved it, you would have received it. You won't achieve anything by whining or making excuses.

Working harder, trying again, and improving yourself are your only remaining options. The deserving person never offers justifications; instead, they just accept the facts and continue their task.

ACCOUNTABILITY IS MUST

You must recognize that life is not always fair, but it will be one day. There are countless stories of people who never gave up and achieved their goals. It's all about consistency, discipline, devotion, obsession, and self-belief in this game. Acceptance is the most fundamental hindrance to people obtaining what they deserve. They refuse to face the facts and instead blame someone else for their failure. They never take accountability for their actions. I want everyone to realize that you are solely responsible for where you are and what you are doing in your life right now, and you deserve it. Your actions and decisions have a significant impact on where you will be in your life in the future.

CHOOSE YOUR CHOICE

You should all be aware of your current life preferences. Your actions and decisions will determine whether you win or lose. If you are an adult, your preference should be to study hard, focus on yourself, learn every day, and become a better version of yourself both physically and mentally. Earn money and get established instead of partying all the time. Quit spending your time with friends who waste your time, stop wasting hours chatting to each other, and stop making girlfriends and boyfriends who are not providing any value to your life. Are you serious about life? Have you ever sat and wondered what your life would be like if you didn't strive for what you wanted? People who strive for what they want in life deserve it and get it, while those who lie on their beds and make excuses don't. You have two choices in life: first and foremost, enjoy your youth and work hard for the rest of your life; or second, work when you are young and enjoy the rest of your life.

FIND YOUR PURPOSE

You must all decide early what you want out of life and what your goal is. We are all here for a certain purpose. You were created for a reason, and there is a cause for your existence. You should be proud that God put you on earth as a human; why do you waste your life by just being average? Everyone has a goal that they want to attain and live their ideal life, but why do only a few get there? The answer is simple and straightforward: they did what they needed, whereas you did not. You were consuming alcohol, regularly partying, smoking, enjoying time with friends, wasting time with your boyfriend or girlfriend, chatting with strangers, watching movies, sleeping for 10–12 hours a day, watching porn, scrolling on social media while they were working hard, going to the gym, sleeping 5–6 hours a day, studying, reading books, learning new skills, working on their business, eating healthy, and giving it their all every day.

SACRIFICE IS INEVITABLE

You might have been there if you had sacrificed all of the temporary pleasures that were diverting you from your goals. Everything you desire to achieve in life requires sacrifice. You must forego all of the joy and fun that your generation is currently experiencing in order to live an incredible future that they will never have. This life is all about mentality and how much you want out of it. You must build a winning environment around yourself, and you must surround yourself with winners. It is definitely true that you become like the individuals with whom you spend the most of your time. Your social network should be made up of people who are eager to succeed in life.

SOME THINGS TO REMEMBER

The world is a giving place; you receive far more than you give. It is impossible for a person to fail if he gives his all every day, strives to improve, works hard regardless of the circumstances, and does not break his promise. Remove the word "excuse" from your vocabulary. Start progressively accepting things, and you will see how much your life will change if you accept responsibility for everything. I encourage everyone who is reading this book to constantly think big in life since mindset affects a lot of things in your life. The way you think determines how you live. The way a person dresses, walks, talks, and thinks may all reveal their personality and qualities.

Everything is accomplished in the imagination before it is accomplished in reality. Nature treats everyone equally, and everyone receives what they deserve and strive for.

SELF BELIEF IS KEY TO SUCCESS

You must understand yourself. Self-belief is one of the most important qualities a person can cultivate in themselves. Many times, individuals are on their way to getting what they deserve, but they lose faith and give up. A great individual is defined by consistency and a never-give-up attitude. Everything has a price, and you must pay it in order to obtain it; similarly, success has a price, and the one who pays the price achieves it. Everything a person has in his life is the product of hundreds of hours of commitment, sacrifices, efforts, discipline, consistency, and many other things. If achieving success was so easy, everyone would have done it.

DISTRACTIONS: PRO OR CON

With all of the distractions in the world, it is extremely difficult to stay focused on yourself, work hard every day, stick to your goals, and maintain discipline. There are two ways to look at this: both negative and positive, Negative individuals will claim that we want to accomplish and be successful in life, but it is tough to stop ourselves from these distractions, which is why we cannot be successful, but positive people will see it as a great opportunity. Most people in today's modern environment lack self-control and discipline. Hence, how simple will it be to become successful if you control your desires, eliminate all distractions, stay focused, and organize your life?

If you learn the skill of self-control, accomplishing your goals will no longer be tough because if most people are distracted, the competition is lessened, and if the competition is reduced, your chances of reaching your goal will naturally improve. Everyone in the world is distracted by many things, such as smoking, drinking, drugs, girls and boys, porn, social media, TV programs, games, and many other things, making it much easier to reach your goals and dreams in today's contemporary world.

YOU WERE NOT WORTHY

You will get what you deserve, and if you get what you do not deserve, it will not last long. Men claim that all women betray and abandon their partners and that they do whatever they want in relationships. She left you because you did not deserve her; you must comprehend why this is happening to you. Let me ask you a question: were you successful, wealthy, or financially dependent? Were you in good shape? Was your personality awesome? Were you a charming, humorous, and masculine guy? You must understand that it is not the fault of women to leave you or cheat on you. The simple answer is that you were replaceable. You were not valuable, and you were unable to fulfil her requirements.

As I previously stated, it is all about player versus player, and you must give your all every day. It's not her fault, believe me. Take yourself to her place. if hundreds of men were sliding into your message box for attention, love, and sex, would your ego not be on top of the mountain because you would have hundreds of options available to you? I am literally telling you, if she finds a better one than you, the game is over, so you need to become a man of your word, set boundaries for her, be strict with her, and don't allow her to disrespect you.

SAME GAME, SAME RULE

You should first become a guy worthy of marrying her, a person with whom she can envision her future, and if she still cheats and does not respect you, it is all her fault. You should leave her with maturity, because a man who understands his value will not take being insulted. Let her know what she has lost. I understand that it is tough to find a woman who is loyal, compassionate, kind, feminine, and ambitious enough to become a wife in today's world, but it is not impossible. You will meet a woman who deserves you, but first you must become a true gentleman who deserves her. The same case applies for women also.

There are also numerous women who claim that, despite our best efforts, our partner cheated on us. Let me ask you a question again: were you loyal, compassionate, and polite to him? Was he the only one with whom you used to talk? Did you try to look better for him? Did you increase his value every time you were alongside him? A man's loyalty is tested when he has everything, whereas a woman's loyalty is tested when her man has nothing.

LOYALTY WORKS DIFFERENTLY, IT IS RARE

So basically, you all need to understand that most individuals only cheat when they have options, and the one who does not cheat when they have other alternatives demonstrates their loyalty. Staying with your partner when you have no other alternatives does not prove your loyalty; loyalty is proved when you have several options but you still choose to stay with that one person. I advise both men and women that if they come across loyalty, they should not allow it go through their hands since it is quite rare these days. It is a difficult concept to grasp, and many women will reject it, but the truth is that most of the time, a man never cheats in a relationship or attempts to leave the girl first; rather, it happens from the woman's side.

According to my prediction, there are a minimal number of incidents where men cheated initially since, as I mentioned before, men do not have options like women, and it is quite difficult for most guys to find another woman.

ARE YOU "THE ONE?"

If a man genuinely loves a woman, he will never cheat on her. There is only one woman in a man's life for whom he will make sacrifices. If you are that woman, he will do everything he can to make you happy and change himself for you, but if a man does not care about your feelings and relationship, then you are not the one he is seeking for. Carefully analyze why your man does not take you seriously. A man desires a woman who is faithful, kind, caring, loving, feminine, and gorgeous. If you lack the traits required to be a wife, change yourself.

A man takes his time determining if you can be his wife or not since you will be the mother of his children. Therefore, a guy is constantly searching for a woman who will understand him and his family and can provide great values for his children. He seeks a lady who can offer love, care, and support in his life, maintain the peace and harmony at home, force him to level up, help him believe in himself when he is down, and stand alongside him in his failures. You will meet someone who truly respects you, but first you must become the lady deserving of becoming a wife.

If you are a loyal, kind, loving, strong, understanding, feminine, and supportive woman and he is still cheating, it is his loss because a true gentleman understands how uncommon a woman like that is. Let him know what he has lost. If a guy does not respect, love, or understand you, leave him because he does not deserve you.

RESPECT IS LOVE

Even if you love your partner very much, you should never stay with them if they don't respect or understand you, since it will always hurt in the long run. If you don't leave them now, there will come a day when you have to truly say goodbye to each other in life, which will hurt even more. Hence, accept your decision and move on since a relationship that lacks love, respect, and understanding won't continue forever and will only give you pain.

> *"It is a man's duty to protect his woman physically, but it is a woman's duty to protect her man spiritually."*
>
> *– Andrew Tate*

To deserve what we want, each of us must first develop that level of capability. I encourage everyone on the entire earth to be the best version of themselves. You only have one life, and you want to squander it like an amateur. Don't you have an inner voice that motivates you to be the best you can be and to live life to the fullest? You will only be able to have that life if you deserve it; therefore, become capable of it as soon as possible and leave footprints for the world to see how lovely life can be if you want it. Regardless of what I say, the final decision will be yours.

8

SOCIETY IS MATRIX

This is going to be a really intriguing and serious topic. Only a few individuals around the globe are rising up and attempting to expose the true reality of the world and the leaders (elites) who have been governing the world according to their preferences for a long time. We are ignorant of the fact that we are not completely free in the society we live in today.

YOUR BELIEF IS FALSE

It is asserted that we are free to make our own decisions, that we have free speech, and that we are free as humans, but the truth is quite the opposite. The government, social media, and the news have all indoctrinated us into believing that we are free to do and say anything we choose. Most of you will now claim, "I am lying, and it is true that we have freedom in every aspect," but you don't comprehend that the individuals who were in the way of the elites and the matrix never survived in life.

People who attempted to raise their voices and step outside the box were banned, executed, removed, and slaughtered. You have two choices: the first is to follow their lead and do as they like, and the second is to reject their falsehoods and strive to prove them wrong in order to reveal their real intentions. What will happen if you select option two? You will be executed or cancelled.

YOU DON'T HAVE YOUR OWN IDEOLOGY

The majority of people have their minds infiltrated by the matrix, which has them programmed to go to school, work hard in class, get a good job, work a 9-to-5 job for their entire lives, save some money for the next generation, and then pass away. You are not in charge of your own thoughts, so you won't be able to comprehend them easily. You are actually under the influence of elites, society, the news, and social media. You behave in accordance with society, speak in the same manner as others around you, listen to what they want you to hear, and watch what they want you to see.

ELITES AND MATRIX

Before delving too far into this subject, I'd like you to be familiar with several phrases and concepts that you might not be familiar with. The world's elites developed the Matrix system to usher in a new, secular world order. The world in which we currently reside is known as the "Matrix," and it is full of deception and fake reality in which the public is not given the dark reality or the true causes of all significant occurrences and incidents around the globe.

The group of people known as the "elites" are above the banks and the government. They are the world leaders who secretly rule the globe.

FROM THE BEGINNING TO THE END

The majority of people in the world are unwilling to embrace the truth because they don't want to acknowledge that others—the news, social media, the school system, false teachings, and elites— have indirect control over their minds and lives. You have been wired with programming since the time of your birth. Your mind begins to subordinate itself to societal beliefs and proverbs. There are many instances, but I'll provide you with a couple to illustrate my point.

Your parents will tell you as you get older that getting wealthy is not our thing since we are middle-class and typical people who can lead fulfilling lives by working a respectable 9-to-5 job and earning average wages. Our professors often tell us that working hard in school is the only way to achieve happiness and success in life. The slave mind cycle and process go like this: attend school, work hard to get good grades, then transfer to a good college or university, finish all assignments, get high grades on all exams, and earn a degree with a high percentage. Then, you apply for jobs, give interviews, and are chosen for good 9-to-5 jobs with good pay. You work hard at your job to get promoted and promoted, save a lot of money for your offspring, and finally, you die. Do you believe that the individual I was portraying was content with his life and had the experiences he wished for? Certainly not, right?

DOES OUR JOB ACTUALLY MAKE US HAPPY?

However, more than 90% of people in our world live this way, and perhaps you are one of them because you are reading this. Can you believe that everything we are taught in school is a lie? They claim that getting a decent job is the only way to become wealthy and happy. Have you ever asked a person who has a 9-to-5 job if they are pleased with their job? Are you living the life you want to live without being under financial strain?

WHY?

Why do society, the world, teachers, and parents convince us that getting a decent job will provide us with a happy and financially free lifestyle when they themselves are not truly happy? Have you ever considered why people still feel that working a 9-to-5 job is everything, even if they are unhappy and dissatisfied with their jobs? Why are parents still forcing their children to continue this cycle of enslavement even if they knew in their hearts that they were not happy in their lives and were unable to meet their needs?

It is because they, like you, were indoctrinated and taught lies, and there are many reasons for this. It is not anyone's fault, but the elites have built the system that allows them to easily manage the brains and brainwash the mindset and attitude according to their choices; by the way, the system is known as school.

THAT'S A GENIUS PLAN

Now, pay close attention to what a superb move they have made and planned. They are convincing parents that they will teach their child all they need to know to help them become a great person in the world. Teachers clearly have influence on children's minds, and eventually parents advise their children to listen to and obey what their teachers say. So, in essence, the education system controls the teachers, and the education system is indirectly controlled by elites. As time passes, the child's mind is programmed, and his or her ability to think beyond the box is erased.

Slowly, friends, family, school, and society convince the individual that becoming wealthy is impossible and that people like us are not cut out for it; everyone gradually demoralizes their mentality to keep it at a certain level. This perspective prevents you from thinking outside the box. It's like locking your mind with a key so you don't try to escape the matrix that the elites have built.

SCIENCE EXPERIMENT

They want to exert mental control over individuals so that they can easily rule the world according to their will. Let me illustrate that for you all with an example: There was a science experiment in which scientists put hundreds of fleas in a jar and closed it for three days. When they opened the jar after three days, they noticed that the fleas were not trying to escape but were instead jumping and flying to a specific level. The reason for this is that they have been trying to jump and fly out of it for three days, and their minds have been conditioned to believe that it is not possible to get out of it because they have been brainwashed into believing that it is not possible to reach there, and the same is happening in schools and universities.

The youngsters are confined in a location where their minds are shaped in such a manner that they are not permitted to think outside the box. They are constantly reminded that just studying and getting a decent job is your destiny, and it is unfortunate to state that more than 90% of the population is slave-minded.

WHY ARE WE TAUGHT THESE THINGS?

However, there are a few individuals who refuse to allow the slave mindset to infiltrate their thoughts and refuse to accept the learning of schools and universities, and these are the people who live their lives the way they want to live. Let me ask you a question: why aren't we taught at school how to earn money, about taxes and investing, how to cope with day-to-day obstacles in life, how to prepare ourselves physically and mentally, and about the skills that will help us grow and earn money? In the end, everyone's goal is the same: to make money. So why is it that the most important element that only matters is not included in the educational system? This should intimidate you into studying subjects that will not assist you in any way in life.

<u>After finishing your studies, you are simply handed a piece of paper that will allow you to show the world your qualifications. Let me tell you something: if you drive a Lamborghini, no one will ask about your qualifications or degree. Nobody will tell you the truth or reality of this dreadful world, but you must analyze everything in your life for yourself.</u>

"The best way to keep a prisoner from escaping is to make sure he never knows he's in prison."

– Fyodor Dostoyevsky

The same thing is happening in schools and throughout the world; we are unaware that we are in a prison where we are bound by the elites and society to stay at a base level in life. We are programmed in such a manner that we do not attempt to break the chain of slavery and poverty so that they can live every minute of their lives and do what they want.

MONEY IS NOTHING BUT STILL EVERYTHING

Money provides you incredible level of freedom and power that you cannot even fathom. Money may not buy happiness, yet everything that brings happiness and satisfaction can only be purchased with money. The smartest move rich people made was to come out in front and tell people that "money does not buy happiness." Many individuals now believe that money does not buy happiness and that money is not everything. Therefore, let me ask you a simple question: why don't wealthy individuals give their whole fortune to charity? How can you be so naive as to assume that money does not bring happiness? Do you believe that the lives of wealthy people are sad and depressing?

YOU ARE NOT HAPPY

The elites convinced you that earning a little money, having a little family, owning an ordinary house, and driving a normal car would bring you happiness, but in reality, this is not the case. Rich people can live their lives to the fullest since they can spend their money as they wish. They travel the world, drive supercars, eat fancy food, and stay in luxurious hotels. Don't you think that their lifestyle makes them happy? Consider for a moment how happy you would be if you were in their situation.

This is the matrix that is deceiving you in order to keep you broke. The world, society, and everything else are designed and structured in such a manner that the elite can control them at any time.

THIS CYCLE NEVER STOPS

People who don't question anything and simply follow the news and media are trapped in the matrix. These types of people are just tools for those who rule the world. If you ever realize how you are being used and brainwashed to become a slave by the elite leaders, you will understand how depressing and difficult normal people's lives are. They repeat the same schedule their entire lives: waking up, bathing, going to work until late at night, getting tired, and then sleeping. Imagine how boring your life will be if you live this way. Most people never get time to be with their families or travel all over the world. Is it not the matrix in which we live? You must accept the truth sooner rather than later, or you will suffer for the rest of your life.

SLAVERY HAS NOT ENDED

It is extremely difficult to escape the matrix since this system has hands in every industry. They own the media companies, the government, the banks, schools, medical institutions, celebrities, and many more. It was designed to enslave the world, and if you believe slavery has ended, you are mistaken. Previously, slaves were forced to work for food and shelter in order to survive and raise a family. In today's society, nothing has changed except that you are now paid for what you do.

Unfortunately, slavery still exists; you have to do what they want you to do; you cannot say no to them because you are still bound in slavery, and the reason is a piece of paper (money) that they can create as much as they want; slavery is not gone; it is still here.

DIVERTED FROM TRUTH

It is very difficult for a normal person to realize and understand the truth because everyone is so preoccupied with fighting amongst themselves, hating society, religious fights, and caste hatred. This is all done on purpose to make everyone self-absorbed and preoccupied, preventing us from thinking beyond ourselves.

Everything we see around us is done on purpose; it is a work of art crafted by a small group of individuals. The system is designed in such a manner that the rich become richer and the poor stay poor; inflation plays a significant part in this. You can easily understand by watching that all the assets, such as private and commercial real estate, land, gold, and businesses, are owned by the rich people, and when inflation occurs, the value of the assets owned by the rich people increases in a large amount, making them more money and making them richer every time, whereas the poor and middle-class people own a vast amount of liabilities, such as cars, houses, bank debt, mortgage debt, interest payments, etc. As they hold liabilities, the value of these things diminishes each year due to inflation, which costs them expenditures and takes their own money away from them, causing the poor to get poorer.

TWO CHOICES, DIFFERENT LIVES

You cannot simply sit and condemn the system; the system will not change; therefore, you must comprehend the rules and discover a method to win and escape the matrix. You can't stop rich people (elites) from getting richer, but you can break the matrix and get rich for yourself and your family. You have two choices: get rich and live like one of them, or remain poor and destitute and become their slave.

Never forget that if you do not have money, you will be a slave to someone who does. If you are not wealthy, you cannot have an opinion since your life is dependent on someone else. Your judgments are not your own; you are under the power of another individual. Being rich is about having freedom in all aspects of life, not only driving supercars, buying expensive items, or having a large house. Money provides you with the freedom to speak and live as an independent human.

EVERYTHING HAS A REASON BEHIND IT

We are in the matrix, and if you start analyzing everything, you will begin to understand how the world works. Nothing happens by coincidence; everything is preplanned. The matrix is everywhere; if you go to the school parking lot and look at the cars your professors and teachers own, you will not find a single car that you would like to drive or own in the future. If the people teaching you about business and economics are not successful in their own lives, how can they teach you to be rich and successful? It's a scam. It is a lot better to use hundreds of thousands of dollars in your business than spend them at the university.

The matrix has created several distractions to keep you all distracted, such as social media, news, television channels, movie platforms, porn sites, and many more. These products are not designed for your pleasure or entertainment, but rather to keep the majority of people occupied.

CREATING A NEW REALITY IN THE WEST

They are preventing individuals from improving and from thinking beyond the box in their daily lives. The movies essentially take away your authentic vision and perspective on the world and transport you to an imaginary realm that does not exist and is far apart from reality.

Teachers in schools are open about sexual subjects, claiming that porn is good and that watching porn and jerking off does not damage, but the fact is quite the reverse. It harms not only our bodies but also our minds, eventually removing our desire and hunger to accomplish things in life. It will lower your testosterone, and as a result, you will start to view women as tools, your human energy will be drained, and you will no longer have genuine feelings as a human being. The worst part is that it will bring regret and shame. The elites want you to be weak because it is much simpler for them to rule the world if men remain distracted, addicted, and weak.

Porn and masturbation will take away your true power; you must examine everything in order to comprehend their motive; their gameplay is much larger than what you think.

MAIN STREAM MEDIA MACHINE

The news channels and media you watch and consume are not in your favor. There is a particular reason why you get all the news from around the world for free; they are not idiots; that they spend billions of dollars on broadcasting and everything else so that everyone can sit at home and listen to what is going on for free. Yes, it is not entirely like that; it is merely used to manipulate you. They also make money via broadcasts and commercials, but you cannot deny the fact that they also use them against you. It's all done on purpose so that they can control all of your brains and influence you the way they want according to their choice. If they can control what they show you, how can they not control your thoughts?

You may not realize it, but you are all controlled by the media; your actions, thoughts, mindset, behavior, personality, and emotions are not yours; you are not in control of your own mind and body; and it is all managed according to the elite's preferences.

DIVIDE AND RULE POLICY

They separated and differentiated us from one another; they divided us into different people—you are black, you are white, you are general, you are OBC, you are men, you are women, and you are gay. These agendas have entirely taken over people's brains and emotions. They did this on purpose so that we would continue to bicker and argue over little matters so that they could sit on top and laugh at us. We were divided into several categories, such as "you are this" and "you are that," but in the midst of it all, we forgot that first and foremost we are humans.

They drove us to battle each other, one family against another, one tribe against another, one caste against another, one religion against another, one gender against another. Do you still think it's not done on purpose? For centuries, they have been indoctrinating us, and they continue to do so today. The majority of people are ignorant that they are being misused by the top leaders. They are projecting things that are not authentic and are far from the truth.

THEY ARE LYING TO YOU

We are offered false assurances that if we slave hard enough for the elites, the end will be lovely and we will be happy with our lives. Earning money is the best way to escape the matrix since it is an essential element. You are free to express your unique beliefs and thoughts if you are financially secure. Without worrying about being forced to a certain level, you can express your views. You can freely express your thoughts and ideas to the entire globe thanks to money. There are certain things that don't matter at all when you have enough money. It's not just about making money; it's also about enjoying freedom.

I advise everyone to do their best to escape enslavement and generational curses since you only have one life and God has given you an opportunity to prove your existence to the world by creating you as a human. You must try your hardest, ignore all negative thoughts, eliminate all distractions from your life, persistently focus on your goals with full dedication, become better every day, begin questioning everything, and realize how important it is to become rich and successful because life is not meant to be lived as a loser.

YOU GOT ONE LIFE TO LIVE

Life is meant to be lived and enjoyed to the fullest extent, with the freedom to participate in a wide range of events at various levels. When one emancipates themselves from the chains of servitude, they unlock the ability to provide assistance and support to their loved ones without hesitation or calculation. If you grasp the truth about the matrix, it becomes extremely impossible to exist without escaping it; therefore, realize it as soon as possible and discover a way out because if you don't, eternal enslavement awaits you.

9

TRUTHS YOU NEED TO ACCEPT

This topic will have an impact on you as a person in every way because I am going to show you the reality of a few things that you must accept as a person because the world is lying to you and everyone is trying to make you weak and manipulate you away from the truth, so I am going to pull four topics and discuss them in detail to prove my points. Read this context with an open mind and a blank slate. Question everything you're about to read here and say to yourself, "Is it true or not?" You will get your answer if you gradually read without any media influence.

1. **BODY SHAMING IS HEALTHY**

2. **DEPRESSION IS NOT REAL**

3. **MASCULINITY IS NOT TOXIC**

4. **MONEY CAN BUY HAPPINESS**

Therefore, we'll go through these subjects in depth and discover the truth behind them. Perhaps I have mentioned them previously, but here I will go into greater depth with a true explanation so that you can all comprehend and embrace the truth. People do not want to hear the truth because they do not want anyone to prove them incorrect, even if their views are unrealistic and delusory.

"No one is more hated than he who speaks the truth."

– Plato

Accepting the truth is always better than fake denial. You've been rejecting it your entire life, even though you know it's true in your heart. Aside from your family and close friends, no one in the world is willing to help you without expecting something in return; they will only do it if they believe you will benefit them in some manner. So how can you believe that the media and society care about your well-being? Always remember that a lie can conceal the truth but cannot alter it.

1.   BODY SHAMING IS HEALHTY

You're probably wondering why I selected this topic first and how it is conceivable that body shaming is healthy. Before you have any negative views about me, read this topic till the end and question yourself. Is this true or not?

Body shaming is the act of criticizing or insulting someone because of their body's shape, size, or appearance. Now I'm going to go into further detail on body shaming. Body shaming is when you criticize or insult someone for things that cannot be altered, such as height, skin color, voice tone, or any disability that cannot be cured or changed. If you shame or mock a person for something that cannot be changed, you are wicked because you do not realize how much anxiety, depression, and mental disorders it causes in a person's life. Put yourself in the shoes of the person you mock, and you will realize how difficult it is for them to confront these types of problems on a regular basis.

Body shaming has a wide range of negative repercussions and consequences in a person's life, including eating disorders, mental health concerns, anxiety, body image disturbance, lower self-esteem, decreased self-confidence, body dysmorphic disorder, sadness, and many more. As a result, humiliating or criticizing someone for things that cannot be altered is a profoundly shameful, disrespectful, and unforgivable act.

> *"If you do not try to change yourself or the circumstance even after being shamed, this shows that you are not really upset about being shamed and are indeed comfortable with it."*
>
> *– Aditya Gupta*

IS IT REALLY HEALTHY? YES

But now I'm going to start proving why body shaming is healthy. Body shaming is 100 percent healthy in terms of things that can be modified, such as body weight, appearance, and many other things. If people start to appreciate and accept that it is okay to be fat or skinny, then no one will attempt to make progress in life because the objective of human existence is to grow and improve with time.

Body shaming is completely healthy for people who want to change their lives, develop themselves, do not want to accept themselves as they are, and always want to become better, but it is unhealthy for people who just want to sit on their bed like a lazy moron, who want to accept themselves as they are, and do not want to become better. These people can achieve nothing in life since they remain the same even after learning the truth. They frequently experience challenges in their daily lives as a result of their personalities and physicality. They still refuse to make a change in their lives, even after knowing that a tiny alteration will entirely turn their lives upside down.

CHANGE IS NECESSARY

For example, if you are obese or skinny and people mock and embarrass you, you should recognize that it is time to make a change in your life. If you go to the gym and get in shape, you will naturally start to look better, and as a result of this shift, all of this mockery and humiliation will stop. People will begin to admire and respect you in life. Understand that you cannot change individuals or society, but you can change yourself. "Body shaming is healthy" for those who accept reality and want to alter themselves, it serves as inspiration and a push to get better.

DIFFERENT IMAPCT ON DIFFERENT PEOPLE

It has a positive impact on an individual's life. There are many people in the world who have transformed because they were body shamed. They altered their lives as a result of the disrespect, judgement, and shame they received from others around them. Therefore, they made the decision that they needed to improve their health, fitness, and overall well-being. When you look at body shaming in a positive way, you will notice that it not only makes you look better and fitter, but it also changes how people talk to you; your confidence level rises; you begin to be respected; your surroundings become healthier (which creates a positive impact in your mind); and people who used to mock you begin to appreciate and believe in you.

Body shaming is detrimental for the majority of people since most individuals do not want to improve their lives and embrace the truth; people will grasp the value of body shaming only when they start improving. Most of the time, body shaming is healthy in terms of appearance because individuals do not realize that they are not always ugly or awful-looking but rather that they need to improve certain specific aspects that will radically transform their entire existence.

PEOPLE DON'T CHANGE UNLESS THEY ARE SHAMED FOR IT

For example, if a person is a 3 or 4 out of 10, he or she can easily become an 8 or 9 by going to the gym, getting in shape, being fit and healthy, changing their fashion sense, trying a new haircut, developing communication skills, taking care of their skin, and changing their walking style. Body shaming plays a vital role in altering all of these traits since most individuals will not change unless they are teased, criticized, and embarrassed throughout their lives. You should come to the decision on your own that I need to transform my life and show everyone who I am; once you have this mentality and attitude, no one can stop you from being your greatest version.

Therefore, we come to the conclusion that body shaming is unhealthy when it comes to things that cannot be altered, but it's healthy when it comes to things that can. You can tell the difference between a winner and a loser by seeing how hard they are working on themselves to make a difference in their lives. Actually, it is harsh to say, but you cannot dispute that not just body shaming, but everything is harmful and useless for those who do not want to improve their lives.

2. DEPRESSION IS NOT REAL

What exactly is depression? According to the internet, depression is a common and serious medical disorder that has a negative impact on how you feel, think, and act. Feeling depressed is real and serious, but the assumption that it will strike you in the head and you will have no control over it is not true.

> *"Depression is not real. Feeling depressed is real. So, you can feel depressed, but you feel depressed and that is a natural, biological, evolutionary trigger for you to change something in your life."*
>
> *– Andrew Tate*

YOU HEAL IT BY YOURSELF

It is not a condition that can only be cured and healed by psychiatrists and psychologists; you are the one who heals it. The world has instilled in you the notion that being depressed is a terrible illness that is extremely hard to conquer. They are convincing you that you are a severe victim of some mental illness that can only be remedied with medicines.

THERE HAS TO BE A REASON

If a person is sad, there must be a legitimate reason for it; no one can become or feel depressed without a problem or a reason. You can't catch depression from the air, and you don't wake up miserable for no reason. You don't comprehend, but the world and psychiatrists are tricking you into believing in things that don't exist.

You cannot be affected by something if you do not believe it. If you believe that depression does not exist, it cannot harm or damage you since you have not allowed it to have an impact on your brain and thoughts. For example, if there are two people in a house and one believes in ghosts and the other does not, if both of them hear a voice in the night from the kitchen of something, the person who believes in ghosts will be scared and will not be able to sleep because of his false idea, but the person who does not believe in ghosts will get up and think that maybe something fell down or maybe it was a rat or the air and go back to sleep.

As a result, depression cannot affect you if you do not allow your mind to believe in it or allow it to stay for an extended period of time. It doesn't mean you can't be depressed; every person faces issues and struggles, but labelling your sadness, failure, anxiety, or problem as depression is pointless.

YOU CANNOT QUIT

Promoting depression as an illness or disorder makes a person weak and helpless. Only you can change the circumstances; no one can change you unless you desire to change. There are many individuals all around the world who are in a worse situation than you. There are people in the world who have lost their entire family in a car accident, and even though they have lost loved ones, they have overcome their grief and pain.

They understand that they cannot change what has happened in the past, but they can influence how their future will unfold. Remember that no matter how bad things get in life, God has kept you alive for a reason.

IT IS A TEMPORARY MENTAL STATE

You have the right to be depressed and sad, but you have to overcome such feelings at some point of time. It is a phase of life that you must encounter one day, but how you handle the situation is entirely up to you. Depression is a temporary mental state that an individual generates for themselves. Do you believe people were not depressed prior to the availability of medications and psychologists? Of course they were, and there were worse issues in the ancient times.

My question is how they were cured previously. I believe that firstly, they were extremely uninformed that depression existed, and secondly, they were aware that no one was there to assist them in overcoming it. Thus, all they did was figure out why they were upset and try to alter their condition; the same thing is occurring now, but people don't realize the reality. Only you can alter the situation; if you keep going forward in life and working toward your goal, one day you will find that it is entirely gone and that it was nothing but your mind that formed a faith and belief in the notion of depression.

LACK OF PURPOSE

Many people suffer from depression because they lack a sense of purpose in life, and this should act as a wake-up call for you to make some adjustments in your life. You can never be depressed when you have speed in your life. Assume you're an obese, broke, and lazy person who spends all day watching TV and eating junk food. Do you think you'll never feel depressed?

Of course, you'll get depressed because one day you'll realize you've squandered your entire life, have no money, are in horrible shape, and have no girls by your side. You now have two choices: either lay on your sofa again, get sad, depressed, weep, regret it, and do nothing, or get out of bed, cut off all distractions, start going to the gym, start your business, hustle hard, acquire new skills, and build your personality. Tell me how you can feel depressed if you choose the second choice. You cannot be depressed if you always work hard, achieve progress in life, and stay in good shape.

ACCEPTING YOUR SITUATION DOES NOT MAKE IT BETTER

Accepting the circumstance is what worsens it. All those who believe they are clinically depressed and believe they need to see a doctor,

I want you to first sit in front of the mirror and ask yourself, "What is the reason or issue that made you think you are depressed?" Then decide whether your reason is genuine or a false perception of yourself, and if it is true, consider what things I need to change in my life to make the situation better. After that, begin focusing on the things that will require you to overcome the current circumstances and never look back in your life.

You will soon realize that what you were dealing with was not an illness or a disorder but rather a phase of life in which you were feeling down and depressed.

PROMOTE POSITIVITY, REMEMBER OTHERS MAY BE IN A LOT WORSE

Every individual has times in his life when he feels sad and weak; therefore, you must understand that this is simply a phase of life that will pass with time. Supporting a person with the idea that he is depressed makes things worse since you are forcing him to realize that he has a major problem and needs someone's support to get out of it.

If you believe your situation is dire, remember that there are children in Syria who face regular bomb explosions, shortages of food, and a lack of water but nevertheless manage to survive. They have no one to share their grief and suffering with. Do you think they're concerned about depression? Let me ask you a question: would you exchange lives with them if given the opportunity? I'm sure you won't. since you understand that their condition is far worse than yours. How can you be depressed if they are not? Have you ever seen or heard a poor man justifying himself to his family or the rest of the world by saying, "I'm feeling depressed; I can't go to work." Of course not, right? He has a harder life and more troubles than you, but he understands that his responsibilities are more important than his excuses. He doesn't have an option but to struggle for his family, so imagine how much better your life is. How can you become hopeless and depressed?

IT IS BOTH A LIE AND A TRUTH

Feeling depressed is real and authentic; you can also feel sad and unhappy; nevertheless, it is a false idea and fallacy to believe that you cannot overcome it. Try to understand that depression is not a serious issue and that it is not acceptable to cry all the time. This false belief just makes you a cowardly and frail person. You must know the difference between the truth and a lie because the world will trap you in their endless fictional notions, therefore you must realize the truth beneath it.

3. MASCULINITY IS NOT TOXIC

What exactly is masculinity? Masculinity refers to the qualities and attributes associated with males or boys. In today's environment, not just women but even men argue that masculinity is toxic, bad for the world, and has a detrimental effect in every way. They claim that in today's world, true masculinity has vanished and only toxic masculinity exists. They are correct about one point: true masculinity is vanishing, and the reason is because the media, news, the world, and even women are all playing a vital role in making men weak and feminine.

THERE ARE TOXIC PEOPLE NOT MASCULINITY

Unfortunately, they are entirely incorrect about considering "masculinity" as being toxic. Let me ask all the women one question: if your house was attacked and you were alone in it without your spouse, would you prefer a masculine, powerful, courageous police officer to come for your help or a weak, feminine, cowardly police officer? Of course, the first one since you know he is the only one who can protect you. Is masculinity toxic for you in this situation?

The elites and the matrix have instilled in women's minds through social media, news, and television that men oppress and overpower them with their toxic masculinity, but the truth is that no husband or boyfriend can touch or even force a woman to do anything without her consent because the man knows how much worse the consequences of his action will be. Hence, try to understand that this false concept of toxic masculinity was created to encourage women to argue with their husbands, insult him, and label him as egoistic and sexist even when he is merely trying to protect his wife from the outside world.

PURPOSEFULLY BOOSTED

The elites purposely popularized the term "toxic masculinity." They propagated it all over the world and shaped minds so that everyone starts believing that masculinity is toxic, and if everyone starts calling men toxic because of their masculinity, men will start to become feminine, weak, and sensitive, due to which men's society will ultimately become helpless. When men become weak, it is very easy for the elites to maintain their control over the world.

WOMEN CAN CHANGE IT

I encourage all women to look deeply inside themselves and consider whether masculinity is really toxic or not. You must determine whether the press and media are truly in your favor. You must analyze whether the press and media are really inclined in your favor. Every woman desires a man who is powerful, brave, physically and mentally strong, capable of protecting her, a dominant man who can make decisions for her and her family, who accepts responsibility for his actions, and who is confident in himself and his purpose (these are the traits and qualities of masculine men).

I am certain that most women love all of these attributes and hope that the man they marry has all of these qualities; thus, how can you state that masculinity is toxic if you desire men like this? The fact is that women adore masculinity in men. Every woman wants a guy by her side who can lead her family, who makes important decisions, makes more money, is more experienced than her, is stronger than she is, is more intellectual and mature than she is. If women appreciate all of these things in men, does that not prove that masculinity is not toxic? Hence, why despise it only because of some media nonsense? So I want every woman to understand what is best for her and not be trapped or deceived by the media or the news.

DON'T LIE ABOUT THE REALITY

I strongly encourage women to never suggest or advertise to men that they can be weak, feminine, kind, or sensitive. If you can't marry a man like him, don't promote these traits; it makes them look weak and gives the incorrect impression.

The majority of women encourage the idea that males can be weak and feminine, and they portray masculinity as a threat; Nevertheless, the moment they sense danger, they begin to seek for a masculine man who is bold, strong, and powerful. Do you think that they want a cowardly, frail, feminine man to appear for their help? Ironically, despite their support for feminine guys and claims that masculinity is unhealthy, they prefer masculine partners. If a fire breaks out in a building, it will take a massive amount of masculinity to save people, and no one will label that masculinity toxic at the same time. It is true that masculine men have fallen short, and one of the primary reasons is mainstream media and news.

YOU GOT ONE LIFE, DON'T DESTROY IT

Ladies, you have no idea how much worse your life will get if you follow this pseudo feminist nonsense. The majority of the women speaking in front of the television are all happily married. They are only repeating what they have been instructed to say. They are attempting to turn you against men by instilling hatred in you. Consider yourself in your 40s, divorced, and living alone with no family. This scenario is a woman's worst nightmare coming true. Imagine dying alone, without a man and a family by your side. Hence, I encourage women to do their best to have a happy family and to consider what is best for them. Even men should understand and respect their partners' sentiments.

PROMOTE MASCULINITY, WEAKNESS IS NEVER APPRECIATED

Masculinity benefits the entire family, so I always encourage men to comprehend that their masculinity is the most attractive quality of themselves and that they should be proud to be masculine. The notion of toxic masculinity by itself doesn't exist. It is the individual who is toxic, not masculinity.

As I already stated, being weak is not an option for a man. Every parent wants a strong son; every sister wants a strong brother; every woman wants a strong husband; and every child wants a strong father.

A man's only option is to be strong. Every family needs a strong father by their side. Never believe the myth that society will embrace you if you are weak and feminine; no one respects or accepts a weak man. Since the dawn of human history, a man has never been appreciated for being weak. You no longer have the luxury of making excuses; you are now an adult. A man who makes excuses is shameless because he continually uses them to cover his failure or laziness.

Being masculine is one of your responsibilities as a guy. Masculinity imposes an obligation on you to do things that are essential to you, even if you do not want to. As a man, you should be disciplined enough to fulfil your daily chores regardless of how you feel. Your emotions should not influence your everyday life, whether you are pleased or unhappy (this is not toxic; it is discipline).

GAMEPLAY IS EVIL

As a man, you must be important, and masculinity plays a crucial role in this process. If you are not important, no one cares about you. The elites want to weaken males because they believe that if they do, then they won't pose a major threat. They are attempting to influence women's minds by demonstrating that women must be masculine and men must be feminine, which is utterly incorrect because going against nature and its norms always results in disaster.

There is a genuine reason why women are born delicate, gentle, and weaker than men; everything has a meaning. The frightening part is that they are propagating within schools, the news, social media, and television that it is okay for a man to be weak, to weep, and to have no control over his emotions.

SELF CONTROL IS ESSENTIAL

Do you know that the most dangerous men on earth are those who lack emotional control and discipline? All of the violence, rapes, robberies, murders, and other crimes are committed by guys who lack emotional control.

Don't embrace the notion of modern civilization; the world requires guys who have emotional control. It is vitally essential for a man to have self-control. You should operate within certain principles, regardless of how you feel. evolve into a guy who does what needs to be done no matter how bad the situation gets. You have responsibilities; there are people who believe in you and rely on you; you cannot let their hopes die. You must protect and provide for your family; you are now an adult. Keep your emotions to yourself; no one cares. It is vital for a guy to be stoic since it provides you the ability to stay calm regardless of the situation; yet, you must grasp the game of emotions.

You must develop the skill of knowing where to display what since you never know what effect your emotions will have on others; this art comes from experience and information gained through time.

ANY CIVILISATION CANNOT SURVIVE WITHOUT MASCULINITY

Men with masculine qualities are fading in today's contemporary environment, which is pushing men to cowardice and weakness. Every country needs men who are strong, powerful, courageous, stoic, dominant, and assertive. Every woman wants a man who can lead, protect her, handle responsibilities, be strong, and provide for their family. Women claim they do not want a violent man, but they do want a man who is capable of violence if they are in a hazardous situation. Society needs men who can sustain the world in peace and harmony. They are pushing this mindset on purpose in order to weaken society and drain men of their manhood. If men are masculine, stoic, and disciplined, the world will be a safer and better place. The world has to realize that being masculine is entirely healthy, not harmful.

4. MONEY CAN BUY HAPPINESS

The world is a matrix, and the elite and wealthy individuals govern it. Before I explain how money can buy happiness, let me show you what money cannot buy.

THINGS MONEY CANNOT BUY

There are a few things that money cannot buy, in my opinion. _The first thing_ money cannot buy is health. A person's body is his own, and no one can improve his health unless he wants to change. No one in this world can buy a fit body and good health; if a person has an issue or problem with his body, he is the only one who can put out the effort to cure it; medicines are merely a support. As a result, even wealthy individuals cannot buy health, making health the first thing that money cannot buy. But there is one exception that I would like to show you all.

EXCEPTIONAL CASE - For example, if there are two people facing the same deadly disease and the first is poor and does not have money while the second is rich and has a lot of money, there is a very rare chance that the first person will survive or not, but the second person has a higher probability of surviving because he will get the best treatment and be treated by the best doctors, so basically money reduces the probability of death. If the person who is rich survives, does that not prove that money can buy happiness? As a result, money is the solution to the majority of problems. In reality, if you have enough money, you can cure more than 90% of diseases.

The second thing that money cannot buy is life. If a person dies, no amount of power or money on the planet can bring them back to life. Death makes no distinction between wealthy and poor; when the time comes, no one can stop it. Death is a harsh reality that everyone must face at some point in their lives, and no amount of money can prevent it, nor can it bring the dead back to life.

Time is _the third thing_ that money cannot buy. There is no amount of money on the planet that can restore the time that has passed. Money cannot buy your childhood or the moment when you were a youngster. You can't go back in time and fix anything.

The fourth thing is family and true love. You cannot buy true and real love; you cannot buy your parents who gave birth to you; you cannot buy family bonds; money can buy the false ones, but it will not bring you happiness since you know they are with you because of your money, and even the love and care would not be real.

The fifth thing that money cannot buy is peace. Money can buy tangible things, but it cannot buy peace of mind. Therefore, while money is a crucial possession that defines a man's success in life, it cannot provide peace of mind. At the same time, it can be said that you can attain happiness and satisfaction while leading a humble life as well.

> *"Money cannot buy peace of mind. It cannot heal ruptured relationships, or build meaning into a life that has none."*
>
> *– Richard M. Devos*

So, in my opinion, these are the few things that money cannot buy. I pondered a lot and tried to think about all I could and came to the conclusion that there is nothing that money cannot buy if we set aside these five things: health, life, time, family, and peace.

THINGS MONEY CAN BUY

Now I'll show you the truth about how money can buy happiness. Money buys freedom, and freedom provides happiness. Every individual desires independence in his or her life, whether physically or financially. Money buys financial freedom, and financial freedom buys endless enjoyment. You have the freedom to dine anywhere you want, to travel the world, to drive supercars, and to purchase anything you want. Will this freedom not bring you happiness?

Money eliminates the restrictions and hurdles that ordinary people face in life, giving you the power that only a few individuals have in this world. True, money provides you with the authority to break certain rules and regulations, and this freedom brings happiness.

Many people believe that money cannot buy happiness; however, the things that bring happiness in life do require money. When you purchase a large house for your family, it brings happiness; when you buy a supercar, it brings happiness; when you travel around the world, it brings happiness; and when you fly in a private jet, it brings happiness. So, in essence, it illustrates that money can buy happiness since most of the things that bring happiness into a person's life can only be bought with money. One of the greatest joys that money can buy is the chance to tell your parents, "You no longer need to work anymore; I will manage everything so that you can live your life the way you want and enjoy it." Will it not bring happiness? Obviously, it will bring happiness.

IT IS CRUCIAL COMPONENT

You all must recognize that money is a crucial component in bringing happiness into a person's life. In today's society, money can be used to acquire even relationships, friends, and even love. Many people would argue that I said the exact opposite in the preceding paragraphs, but try to realize that I was speaking about true love and real family connections.

Let me give you an example: when you don't have any money, many of your friends leave you, your partner (the love of your life) abandons you, and you start to lose people; but, when you become successful and wealthy, the people who abandoned you in your darkest time return into your life. They all start respecting, appreciating, and praising you all of a sudden, and sometimes your partner returns to apologize for leaving you. Do you think they returned because they realized their mistake and realized how important you were? Of course not, but the true reason is because you are now wealthy and successful, which proves that money can buy friendship and love.

DOES IT OR DOES IT NOT

The notion that "money does not buy happiness" came from elites and rich people. They made a brilliant and outstanding move by stepping forward and telling people that money does not buy happiness. Due to this concept, people begin to think that having money is not necessary to be happy, and by using this tactic, they divert people's attention and reduce their desire for money.

I don't see how people can be so stupid as to accept it. Let me ask you a question: if money cannot buy happiness, why do the rich and elites not donate or give away their whole fortunes? Even after earning so much money, why do they continue to earn more? The truth is that people were misled so that they would not try to earn more money, making it possible for the rich and powerful to keep everything. Try to understand that it is all done for a purpose.

MONEY DOESNOT STEAL HAPPINESS

It is false that the wealthy and privileged are sad, that their families are unhappy, that they are perpetually depressed, and that they do not have pleasure in life. Try to question everything in the world and understand the truth behind it since you have constantly been lied to. Money is an extremely vital element of life. It is similar to water in that it will not make you happy in and of itself, but if you go without it for an extended period of time, you will begin to need it. Do not allow anyone to convince you that money cannot buy happiness; there are individuals in the world who have the finest lives. Try to understand that it is possible to have the best possible life. There are people in the world who are wealthy, successful, and happy, with a lovely family and a luxurious lifestyle.

10

KNOW WHERE YOU HAVE BEEN LIED TO

You need Morpheus to escape the matrix since the modern world has destroyed and brainwashed most people's minds into thinking things that are not true.

The news and social media are significant players in this, causing men and women to adopt false ideas and believe in lies. The matrix and its participants are trying everything they can to manipulate men, women, and society. You can influence people's minds by controlling what they see, hear, and talk. Only the elite have this power. People throughout the world use social media and watch the news. All of these things are controlled by the elites. Therefore, if they can control what you see and hear, they can easily control your mind and influence you.

FORCING YOU TO BELIEVE

People all across the world are progressively compelling each other to believe in the agenda displayed by the media and news. If you dig deep and question everything, you will discover that you were being deceived the entire time. Have you ever pondered why you get to use social media and watch news for free? It's all on purpose. Not just the elites but also the environment in which you live are constantly misleading you.

THE STORY FULL OF LIES

Nobody desires for you to surpass them in money and success. you're on your own on this journey; hence, you need to comprehend and know where you're going. In this topic, I will expose the lies that the media, news, and the world tell to all people.

"The naked truth is always better than the best-dressed lie."

– Ann Landers

The first and most important lie they are teaching us is that <u>men do not need women and women do not need men.</u> They are instilling conflict between men and women by overpowering and influencing agendas such as toxic masculinity, feminism, inequality, and oppression against women. They are also pushing forward the false belief that men have all the power and money, whereas women are victims. I discussed this context in one of my topics. The elites and inhabitants of the matrix seek to divert everyone's attention so that conflicts between men and women continue without anybody realizing the true cause of the conflict.

BREAKING THE FAMILIES

They are convincing us that we do not need each other, and as a result, divorce rates are increasing, household disputes are on the rise, loyalty is diminishing, and partners are cheating on each other. One of the primary reasons for all of this is the notion that "men and women do not need each other," and as a result of this thinking, people begin to lose regard for their partners, and when you lose respect, love dies because respect represents love in a relationship. They desire men and women to continue fighting with each other.

I'm not sure why, but the media has had a detrimental impact on young women in the West, and it is quickly spreading to other nations. You will find a lot of women out there stating that they don't need men, but the funny thing is that you will not find a single man saying that I don't need a woman. Women are easier to manipulate than men, and the media is exploiting women as a tool to instill hostility in society.

USING WOMEN AS A TOOL

Their major goal is not to make women independent; rather, they are exploiting women as a weapon to achieve their goal of breaking down civilization. They are destroying the love and tranquilly within families. They are brainwashing and encouraging women to believe that men do not want women to work and progress, and as a result, we witness protests and disputes between men and women, not just in the workplace but also in homes, streets, and many other places. Most women do not realize that the truth is just the opposite.

EACH OF US IS BETTER AT CERTAIN THINGS

In the modern world, if you ask men whether they support allowing women to work or not, they will tell you that they are strongly in favor of it. I am confident that you will not find a single man who believes that women should not be permitted to work. Every man wants to see his wife succeed in life. God made each of us uniquely different from each other for a reason.

We are both better at some things as men and women; there are few things that men can do better than women, and there are few things that women can do better than men. In society, we each have unique tasks and responsibilities. We should have the guts to admit that men and women specialize in different things, that we each have distinct strengths and weaknesses, and that there is nothing wrong with embracing our respective positions. God made us uniquely diverse so that we might identify with and strengthen one another's shortcomings.

TOGETHER WE ARE UNSTOPPABLE

The media and society are doing their best to spread the idea that men and women are the same, but you need to realize that we are really different from one another. Although we need to be treated equally, this does not imply that we can outperform one another in particular areas. Since we are discussing the majority in this case, exceptions do not apply. Men are better at giving protection, just as women are better at raising children. Therefore, we must acknowledge that each of us is better suited for particular roles. If we work together, we can become an unstoppable force on this planet. It will foster mutual understanding among us, enabling us to have a beautiful and content family.

NEED EACH OTHER SURVIVAL

For humanity to survive, we are all necessary. Men cannot create life, but women can, and God has endowed them with the wonderful chance to do so. As I previously stated, women can better care for children and men can better guard the family; therefore, we must acknowledge that we require each other at different stages of life and that we are dependent on each other. We are incomplete without one another; we are equal halves that become whole when we team up. Denial by any individual or group will not alter the truth. We were, are, and will continue to be essential to each other's lives and existence.

YOU ARE OUT OF TIME

The second lie they tell is that _there is ample time to accomplish things and that you can relax and enjoy life._ They've been lying to you, and they're lying to you again. Elites tell people that it is okay to be ordinary, that it is okay to be broke, that it is okay to take it easy in life, and that there is enough time. There are many individuals who listen to this advice and believe it. "I highly advise everyone not to trust in things that take away their power." You don't realize how short life is; they've been lying to you the entire time.

Since you only have a limited amount of time on Earth, you must recognize that you must act quickly. _Speed is everything;_ you must realize early on that you do not have enough time to become successful; you are in your early twenties and still chilling and partying. There will be plenty of time to enjoy life afterwards, but first become established, wealthy and successful as soon as possible, because there is no liberty in driving supercars in your fifties.

TIME IS THE REAL MONEY

You may not realize it, but it is difficult out there; the world is too harsh for those who lack value and status. If you do not value your time and squander it, you will learn at some point in your life that there is not enough time and that you are being misled.

When you reach the age of 30, you will realize the value of time because you will be alone in life, without any friends, and without any money. It will be a very depressing and difficult period of life to get through. I want everyone to make the most of their time, since time is money. You all must recognize one truth: you can earn money again, but you cannot recover lost time. Understand their technique for making you lethargic, weak, and poor. Do you believe all the rich and famous individuals thought, "I have ample time; I'll do my work next week," or that they rested and slept for weeks because they were tired? Certainly not! They worked their butts off, they gave their all every day, they didn't take breaks, they weren't lazy like you, they didn't make excuses, and they realized I didn't have enough time and I needed to be successful and wealthy as soon as possible to enjoy my dream life.

"Once you stop exchanging time for money, you will understand the true value of time."

– Aditya Gupta

PERSON WHO DOES NOT TAKE REST > WHO TAKES REST

As I previously stated, try to question everything you see or hear since most of the time, what you see or hear is not to your advantage. The person who does not take breaks in life, does not waste time, works harder every day regardless of how he feels, does not make excuses, and always strives to be the best version of himself will always be more successful and wealthy than the person who takes breaks, makes excuses, wastes time, is lazy, and does not work hard.

It is a battleground, and you must become the best player in order to survive.

Always challenge yourself, strive to learn new things, get better every day, focus on yourself, and most importantly, stay disciplined. Allow nothing into your life that will lead you to become weak. You only have one life, and if you can't accomplish your aspirations in that life, shame on you.

SATISFACTION KILLS GREATNESS

The next lie they teach you is that _you should be satisfied with what you have._ People who are pleased with their current circumstances are unlikely to achieve great things in life. Satisfaction is a roadblock to success in life. All of the great people in history that you know and have heard of were people who were never satisfied in life. If you ask the greatest athlete or artist if they were satisfied with their lives, the answer will be no. Have you ever seen a wealthy person get satisfied with what they have? No, not at all! because they understand that never being satisfied in life will make them great. For example, in today's society, who does not know Elon Musk? He is one of the world's richest individuals and has accomplished far more in life than the average person. But have you ever seen him stop working? Of course not! If the world's richest guy isn't satisfied with what he has, how can you all be satisfied with what you have?

ALWAYS STRIVE FOR EXCELLENCE

Every great person had the choice of being satisfied with what they had in life, but if they were satisfied with what they had previously, you would not have known about them. Their names would have been ordinary, and they would not have been remembered for a long period of time.

I'm not saying you shouldn't be satisfied with what you've accomplished in life; it's vital to appreciate and be proud of yourself when you do. Looking back and seeing how far you have come in life with your devotion and hard work is one of the most wonderful feelings. According to me, a person should celebrate his or her accomplishments and successes in life from time to time but never get satisfied with them since something bigger and greater is waiting up there. Many people confuse appreciation with satisfaction, but it is crucial to acknowledge that they are two quite different things.

THIS CHOICE SEPARATES THE GREATEST PEOPLE FROM AVERAGE

You have two choices in life: be satisfied with what you have and live a regular life as a normal person, or never be satisfied at any point in life and live the best possible life as the greatest person. The greatest individuals in history did not have the term "satisfaction" in their vocabulary. Satisfaction kills greatness and hunger inside a person; it prevents a person from progressing in life because when you are satisfied with what you have, you do not want more. The matrix and the elites want everyone to be satisfied with what they have; they want to fully eliminate people's hunger for money and power because if people are satisfied, it would be much simpler for them to control the globe and have all the power and money.

DEVELOP YOUR MIND FROM ZERO

If you try to comprehend this system, you will be astounded by what they have constructed and what they have done to the globe. The astonishing thing is that it was created by only a few people. You cannot break this system, as I have often stated, but you can escape it. You must entirely shift your mentality since you have been deceived from the beginning. Your mentality will not change overnight, but as time passes, you will have to analyze everything and figure out why. With time, you will gradually learn the reality behind these ideas and beliefs.

DISCIPLINE IS THE KEY TO SUCCESS

The fourth lie they tell you is that *you must be motivated to succeed in life.* Let me tell you something: motivation isn't real; it's just a prediction of our own behavior. The relationship between say and do is a distinct topic.

You may claim to be motivated under specific circumstances but never follow through. Alternatively, assume you are demotivated in the same conditions but still get the job done. Motivation is not a stable and real concept since people declare they are motivated but do not complete the task despite having enough motivation. Discipline is real, while motivation is fake. For example, there are two people who go to the gym: one who is motivated and one who is disciplined. The guy who is motivated will only go to the gym when he feels motivated. When he lacks motivation to go to the gym, he will skip it (basically, it depends on his mood), while a disciplined person would go to the gym every day regardless of how he feels. It makes no difference to him whether he is happy or sad; he understands that he has to do what he is supposed to do. The second individual will always triumph over the first.

DISCIPLINE IS PERMANENT

A motivated person has never been successful in life, but a disciplined one has. Motivation is unstable and can break at any time, but discipline is stable as it builds consistency. Discipline requires a lot of effort, and discipline is crucial to building a successful individual.

Discipline carries a force that motivation does not; sentiments are irrelevant to a disciplined individual. It makes no difference to him if he has a headache or is depressed. A disciplined individual is aware of his responsibilities and will carry them out. Motivational videos will not help you unless you don't want to work. Motivation is temporary, but discipline is permanent. Choose discipline over motivation every time. The matrix wants you to be locked in a false thought that does not work; they want you to be weak. They do not want disciplined warriors who understand their worth, but rather motivated puppets that perform according to their desires and lack the ability to think for themselves.

They have been programming us since the beginning of time, using all of us as tools until now. You must all break the chain of servitude and escape the matrix.

SLAVE CYCLE CONTINUES FOREVER

The fifth lie they tell you is that <u>working from 9 to 5 will make you happy.</u> They have trained the minds of more than 95 percent of people to believe that you are built for 9 to 5 and that this is all you need in life. Do you honestly believe that a person who works 9 to 5 is happy in his life? Sorry to say, but that is not realistically possible; a person who is a slave to the matrix can never be happy in his life, as I will demonstrate to each and every one of you with an example. A person who drives a normal bike or car, earns a few dollars, lives in a normal house, has an average-looking wife or husband, and travels once a year can never be happy.

"Slaves are never born by birth; They are always created through a slave mindset."

– Aditya Gupta

JOB DOES NOT MAKE YOU HAPPY

Everyone wishes to live the life of a rich individual at some point in their lives. It is a myth that jobs make people happy. Everyone in our world understands that working 9 to 5 can only fulfil your requirements, not your dreams. The matrix and the elites aim to create slaves who don't question anything and simply follow commands. 9 to 5 is one of the finest ways in the world to manufacture slaves since most of them are aware that they are replaceable and have no other options in life.

They want you all to become their slaves and operate like machines, so you just obey their orders, act like robots, and follow their orders blindly without your own will. They merely use you as a tool now and then and replace you when they find a better one. Slavery is not gone; it is still here. In the past, the government would obtain slaves and force them to labor for free according to their desires (this is slavery) in exchange for food and shelter. What is occurring now is still the same, but the only change is that individuals are now paid for their jobs, and they receive money to spend on food and housing.

FALSE SATISFACTION

Nothing has changed; try to grasp reality. Ignoring the truth won't alter anything; the truth will stay the truth, and the lie will remain the lie. Reality cannot be denied. People who claim that they are satisfied with their jobs are lying. They refuse to acknowledge the fact that they want a different life than the one they have now. The reason is that they want to give themselves a fake sense of satisfaction that would make them feel happy. You must all believe in yourself and ponder how you can become wealthy and successful in life since this is the only way to experience true freedom and pleasure in this contemporary society. It is quite tough to lead a normal life and stick to the same pattern every day.

WHY CAN'T YOU

Life is not just about survival; it is also about enjoying every single moment. You may not realize it, but 90% of the things in the world can only be enjoyed if you have enough money to spend. I don't understand how individuals don't have the desire to succeed and conquer life. You must all break free from the slave cycle of 9 to 5; you were not born to acquire a job, work for someone else for 30 years, develop their empire, and then die; this is not the life you deserve. Look at yourself; you have warrior blood; your ancestors did not survive all the calamities, diseases, wars, and disasters for you to live an ordinary life. Why don't you want to be one of the one percent of individuals who live the finest life they can? Don't you believe you deserve that type of life? We are all the same; we are all humans, and if someone else can do it, why can't you? You are not different from them.

There are many more falsehoods to tell, and it is impossible to describe them all in one topic, but I did my best to show you all 5 big lies that the matrix and the elites tell you all the time. It is impossible to reveal and explain every lie since there are thousands of them; therefore, you must comprehend and question everything because this world is a trap and you are in the matrix, Neo.

www.ingramcontent.com/pod-product-compliance
Lightning Source LLC
Chambersburg PA
CBHW022018150726
47990CB00002B/705